GET BETTER
OR
GET BEATEN!

31 Leadership Secrets from GE's
Jack Welch

ROBERT SLATER

Professional Publishing
Burr Ridge, Illinois
New York, New York

This publication is designed to provide accurate and authoritative information in regard to the subject matter covered. It is sold with the understanding that neither the author nor the publisher is engaged in rendering legal, accounting, or other professional service. If legal advice or other expert assistance is required, the services of a competent professional person should be sought.

From a Declaration of Principles jointly adopted by a Committee of the American Bar Association and a Committee of Publishers.

Editor-in-chief:	Jeffrey A. Krames
Project editor:	Jane Lightell
Production manager:	Jon Christopher
Interior designer:	Mercedes Santos
Cover designer:	Tim Kaage
Compositor:	Alexander Graphics
Type face:	11/13 Palatino
Printer:	Book Press, Inc.

Library of Congress Cataloging-in-Publication Data

Slater, Robert (Robert I.)
    Get better or get beaten! : 31 leadership secrets from GE's Jack Welch / Robert Slater.

    p. cm.
    ISBN 0-7863-0235-6
    1. Leadership.   2. Industrial management.   3. Competition.
I. Title.
HD57.7.S57   1994
658.4'092—dc2O   93-44767

Printed in the United States of America
3 4 5 6 7 8 9 0 BP 1 0 9 8 7 6 5 4

FOREWORD

John F. Welch, Jr., known to most as Jack, became General Electric's eighth and youngest chief executive officer and chairman in April 1981. He was 45 years old.

He was born November 19, 1935, in Peabody, Massachusetts, across the city line from Salem, where he grew up.

He graduated from the University of Massachusetts at Amherst with a degree in chemical engineering. The following year he received a master's degree in engineering from the University of Illinois; in 1960 he obtained his doctorate from the University of Illinois.

He began working for General Electric in Pittsfield, Massachusetts, building its plastics unit into a multibillion-dollar business. In late 1971 Welch became general manager of the Chemical and Metallurgical Division.

A year later he was made vice president. In 1973 he became vice president and group executive of the components and materials group. Welch was later given other businesses to manage apart from plastics, including medical systems and diamonds.

In December 1977 he was promoted to senior vice president and sector executive of the Consumer Products and Services Sector and vice chairman of the GE Credit Corporation. In August 1979 Welch was made one of three GE vice chairmen.

He became chairman and CEO of GE in April 1981. Presiding over a corporation that most had thought to be successful, Welch radically reshaped General Electric, pioneering the now-routine business techniques of restructuring and downsizing.

In 1981 GE was only 10th in market value among American public companies. In 1993 GE, with roughly $80 billion in market value, shared the lead with Exxon and AT&T.

To revive General Electric during the 90s, Welch sold $12 billion and purchased $26 billion worth of businesses.

Along the way, Welch pared GE's workforce from 412,0000 to only 229,000.

In the early 1980s, only three GE businesses—lighting, motors, and power systems—led their markets. Only aircraft engines and plastics were global.

In 1993 12 of the 13 GE businesses were number one or number two in their markets. (NBC was the lone exception).

At the start of Welch's leadership, each GE business had 9 to 11 organizational layers; a decade later that figure was cut to 4 to 6.

Annual corporate productivity rose from 2 percent in 1981 to 4.5 percent in 1993.

General Electric had, at the start of the 1980s, $25 billion in sales and profits of $1.5 billion. In 1993 the company had revenues of $60.6 billion and net earnings of $5.2 billion.

General Electric is considered the most successful corporation in America.

And, by virtue of his vision and his remarkable achievements, Jack Welch has became America's most-respected chief executive officer.

CONTENTS

LEADERSHIP SECRETS

1
CHANGE, BEFORE IT'S TOO LATE!

2
LOOK REALITY IN THE EYE AND DON'T FLINCH!

3
BE READY AND EAGER TO REWRITE YOUR AGENDA!

FROM THE FILES OF Jack Welch

"The mind-set of yesterday's manager was to accept compromise and keep things neat, which tended to breed complacency. Tomorrow's leaders, on the other hand, raise issues, debate them, resolve them. They aren't afraid to go against today's current because they know their constituency is tomorrow. They rally around a vision of what a business can become."

What is the best way to succeed in business?

If all of us knew the answer—or answers—to that question, how fortunate we would be.

If only we could say: "Follow these leadership secrets, and your company will earn greater profits."

There is lots of advice out there, lots of people offering those secrets.

Let's, however, be realistic.

It's terribly hard to know which advice to take, which to avoid.

One approach—the one we recommend—is to look at the very best, hone in on the business ideas that seem to be the most effective.

In this case, the very best business ideas belong to a man named Jack Welch.

THE CHAIRMAN AND CHIEF EXECUTIVE OFFICER OF GENERAL ELECTRIC

Welch's track record is the envy of every CEO in America. He has won "CEO of the Year" honors a number of times. General Electric has been touted as the most successful company in the United States.

He took GE from sales of $25 billion in 1981 to $60.6 billion in 1993 and made it one of the most profitable companies in America.

He turned GE into what *Forbes* magazine called "the most powerful enterprise in American business."

We can do no better than to focus on the business ideas of Jack Welch. In the following pages, we will spell out Welch's ideas in great detail.

Let's keep one thing in mind.

When Jack Welch talks about the business ideas that he has employed in moving General Electric forward, he is talking about business ideas that are applicable for managers of any corporation, small, middle-sized, or large.

So, let's pay careful attention to Jack Welch's 31 leadership secrets for competing successfully in business.

His track record demonstrates that his business ideas work for General Electric.

Unquestionably, there is a great deal to be learned from him.

Of all the business ideas Jack Welch has espoused, none is more important than this one:

CHANGE, BEFORE IT'S TOO LATE!

"No one likes change," says Welch. "They all start off with, 'I like the way things are. That's why I'm here. If I didn't like the way it is, I'd be somewhere else.' "

Change.

It seems easy enough to do.

One decision from the boss. Getting the employees to alter their patterns of behavior.

Discarding an old way. Adopting a new one.

Easy, right?

Not at all.

It may well be the hardest thing for anyone in business to do.

Welch knows this. But he has been advocating change as a business rule from the first day he took over as chief executive of GE in the spring of 1981.

Unlike many other business leaders, Jack Welch understood the perils that faced large corporations like GE during the 1970s and 1980s.

He sensed that the business environment was going through rapid and major changes, changes that could have had disastrous results for GE and other major companies.

At the start of the 1980s, so much was new: High-tech industries and global competitors were sprouting up; higher-quality products and new standards of productivity were appearing.

And it was all happening at a much faster pace than ever before.

The heads of other corporations found these changes irrelevant and hard to understand.

Even if they had sensed how crucial it was for their companies to reshape themselves—because of that new environment—they hated change.

Welch, on the other hand, recognized that one could not avoid change. He welcomed the opportunity to put General Electric through important alterations.

He welcomed it because he knew the importance of another vital business rule:

LOOK REALITY IN THE EYE AND DON'T FLINCH!

Without facing reality, it was impossible to stay competitive, impossible to win.

The winners won **because they assessed their opponents' strengths and the playing field accurately.**

The losers fell by the wayside **because they stuck their heads in the sand.**

To be a winner, according to Jack Welch's leadership secrets, business leaders (he dislikes the word *manager*) should wake up each day as if it were January 1. As he says:

BE READY AND EAGER TO REWRITE YOUR AGENDA!

4

MANAGING LESS IS MANAGING BETTER

*"A*s we became leaner, we found ourselves communicating better, with fewer interpreters and fewer filters. We found that with fewer layers we had wider spans of management. We weren't managing better. We were managing less, and that was better."

When Jack Welch articulates his thoughts, the business community listens.

Part of the reason is the immense success GE has had since Welch became its leader.

Part of the reason is the great respect businesspeople have for General Electric.

General Electric is the company that **Thomas Edison** helped to found, the world-famous corporation that has been the provider of light bulbs and aircraft engines, locomotives and medical imaging equipment, and countless other products.

Just as importantly, GE has long been respected within the business community for its innovations not only in product lines, but also in management technique.

When GE developed a new management style, that style was often emulated by many others in American business.

When the company decentralized in the 50s, it was no surprise that **decentralization** became the wave of the future.

When GE built up immense bureaucracies in the 60s and 70s, countless other enterprises accepted the idea that largeness was a virtue in the business world.

Now, in the 1990s, thanks to the business precepts of Jack Welch, General Electric is once again providing a **role model for American business**.

Welch has given American business leaders a **new outlook on how to manage**.

Or, more aptly, how not to manage.

In arguing that

MANAGING LESS IS MANAGING BETTER

Welch has set a new style for the management of the large American corporation.

He started the decade of the 80s by **discarding senior management**, enabling him to talk directly to the leaders of his businesses.

He called the discarding of those senior managers

DELAYERING.

But, even that, he found, was not sufficient.

To make General Electric competitive, he put the company through a change greater in scope than any ever undertaken in a major American corporation.

In doing so, he became the pioneer of a process that until then had no name. Today it is called

RESTRUCTURING.

5

TAKE A HARD LOOK AT YOUR OVERALL
BUSINESS, AND DECIDE AS EARLY AS
POSSIBLE WHAT NEEDS FIXING,
WHAT NEEDS TO BE NURTURED,
WHAT NEEDS TO BE JETTISONED!

"The world is moving at such a pace that control has become a limitation. It slows you down."

Only a decade before Jack Welch took over as chief executive officer (in April 1981), General Electric was steaming full-throttle for a crisis that almost no one acknowledged.

Just a handful of General Electric's 150 business units were number one or number two in their markets (lighting, power systems, and motors).

Plastics, gas turbines, and aircraft engines were the only GE businesses doing well overseas. And only gas turbines had market leadership overseas.

Despite gleaming balance sheets in the 1970s, GE appeared **headed for the shoals**.

As late as 1970 as much as 80 percent of General Electric's earnings still came from its traditional electrical and electronic manufacturing businesses. Yet manufacturing was on the slide.

The company's successes were plastics, medical systems, and financial services. But these businesses contributed only one-third of the total 1981 corporate earnings.

Finally, a number of GE's businesses such as aircraft engines often used up more cash than they produced.

GE's troubles were linked to the changing global business environment.

In former times, America had held sway over the most important markets of the world economy, whether in steel or textiles, shipbuilding or television, calculators or automobiles.

Then, with few taking notice, others, especially the Japanese, started to take away clients, seducing them with **higher-quality products at cheaper prices**.

Smokestack America was crumbling, and one dismal sign was in the steel industry, which in 1982 lost $3.2 billion. In parallel, the Japanese had grabbed 20 percent of the American market. What was happening in steel was felt as forcefully in the American car industry.

America's consumer electronics industry also failed to read the signals coming from across the Pacific. By the time it understood that Americans had a voracious appetite for videocassette recorders it was too late. The Japanese had cornered the market from the start.

With the arrival of the 1980s, the American economy looked increasingly unhealthy. Inflation, only 3.4 percent in 1971, had climbed to 18 percent in March 1980.

Other signs of distress were in evidence.

The price of oil, only $1.70 per barrel in 1971, peaked at $39 per barrel in 1980.

Auto and truck production, reaching 8 million vehicles in 1971, slid to a mere 6.4 million by 1980.

Still the highest in the world, American productivity outpaced the West Germans and the Japanese in 1979; yet it had been slowing since the 60s.

In 1979 the United States ranked only 10th in annual per capita income ($10,662) among members of the Organization for Economic Cooperation and Development.

Not surprisingly, America headed for a recession in the summer of 1981.

The United States had to become not only **more productive**, but also **more aggressive** in competing for business around the world.

World trade stood at $2 trillion in 1981 and was expected to grow dramatically over the decade. Yet thousands of American companies were not exporting.

Only 1 percent of American firms accounted for 80 percent of the country's exports.

Nine out of 10 American companies did not export at all.

Jack Welch's business ideas were a response to the changes in the global business environment.

The changes had come slowly, almost imperceptibly.

Before, only the American marketplace had counted: The remainder of the world economy appeared inconsequential. It was possible for companies like General Electric to flourish.

Yet, by the 1970s, changes were occurring. The **"rest of the world"** no longer seemed microscopic, irrelevant.

Welch, however, sensed correctly that the business arena had been growing **larger and increasingly competitive**: A whole new array of enterprises with international pretensions were popping up around the globe.

Jack Welch recognized all of these momentous changes long before others did.

When he became the chairman and chief executive officer of GE in the spring of 1981, **he could have pretended**

- The 115-year-old business icon over which he was about to preside would continue to sell its light bulbs and refrigerators and turbines regardless of the changes occurring in the American business environment.

- GE, with its 350 business units, was so diversified, so solid, so capable of absorbing the ups and downs that were normal to any economy, that little could bother the company's steady financial climb.

HE COULD HAVE CHOSEN TO STICK HIS HEAD IN THE SAND.

BUT HE DID NOT.

Only by acting, by reshaping the corporation, did he believe there was a chance that General Electric would emerge stronger in the 1980s and 1990s.

Welch alone believed that a **revolution** was needed inside GE to weather the stormy ocean of economic and competitive challenges.

For companies like GE **to survive** in such a rapidly shifting environment, a **whole new vision** was needed, an entire **new set of business strategies**.

Others inside GE and outside scoffed at Welch. They insisted changes were not needed, that in time all would be well.

After all, this was a company that at the start of the 80s had been generating $25 billion in sales—and $1.5 billion in profits.

GE employees and business analysts alike greeted him at first with disdain and disbelief and outright fear.

Here was someone tampering with sacred tradition, fixing something that was not broken, playing with fire.

And yet, had other business leaders acted as Jack Welch did, had they followed one of his most important leadership secrets, they might well have avoided the crises that afflicted their companies in the early 90s.

That secret—Jack Welch's leadership secret 5—was this:

TAKE A HARD LOOK AT YOUR OVERALL BUSINESS, AND DECIDE AS EARLY AS POSSIBLE WHAT NEEDS FIXING, WHAT NEEDS TO BE NURTURED, WHAT NEEDS TO BE JETTISONED!

Jack Welch had a gut instinct that **something needed fixing**.

> *I could see a lot of (GE) businesses becoming . . . lethargic. American business was inwardly focused on the bureaucracy. (That bureaucracy) was right for its time, but the times were changing rapidly. Change was occurring at a much faster pace than business was reacting to it.*

Others saw the virtue of a decentralized organization. But Jack Welch saw only chaos.

Others found orderliness in GE's bureaucracy. Welch complained that the company's bureaucracy was excessively sluggish.

Others were convinced that layers upon layers of management created the best possible command-and-control system.

But to Welch, those layers were merely wasting precious time and spinning their wheels, losing sight of their basic purpose.

> *The old organization was built on control, but the world has changed. The world is moving at such a pace that control has become a limitation. It slows you down. You've got to balance freedom with some control, but you've got to have more freedom than you ever dreamed of.*

Because it had businesses in so many different fields, General Electric was bound to be affected by what was going on across the oceans.

CLEARLY, IT WAS TIME TO DIVERSIFY.

CLEARLY, IT WAS TIME TO MOVE THE COMPANY INTO DIFFERENT DIRECTIONS.

Welch's goal?

To make General Electric the most competitive enterprise on earth.

> *A decade from now we would like General Electric to be perceived as a unique, high-spirited, entrepreneurial*

enterprise . . . a company known around the world for its unmatched level of excellence. We want General Electric to be the MOST PROFITABLE, HIGHLY DIVERSIFIED COMPANY ON EARTH, with world-quality leadership in every one of its product lines.

That was Jack Welch talking to his board of directors and share owners on April 1, 1981, the date he took over as CEO and chairman.

If GE could be revived, there seemed to be hope for other major corporations—in autos, steel, and banking.

Welch was ready. He was eager to put his business ideas to work, to test them, to determine which ones were valid, which ones were not. He would shape and refine his ideas over the next decade, a decade in which General Electric grew into the most successful company in America.

6

FACE REALITY!

7

DON'T PURSUE A CENTRAL IDEA BUT, RATHER, SET ONLY A FEW CLEAR, GENERAL GOALS AS BUSINESS STRATEGIES.

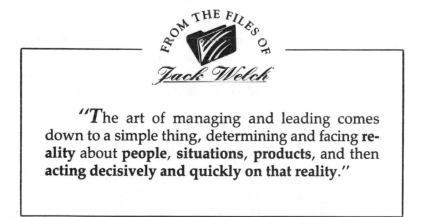

"The art of managing and leading comes down to a simple thing, determining and facing **reality** about **people, situations, products**, and then **acting decisively and quickly on that reality**."

If a company was out of touch with the business environment, its only salvation lay in undertaking a radical change.

The radical change that Jack Welch employed was called

RESTRUCTURING.

At that time restructuring was a new idea. The word had not yet come into vogue.

It did not mean stripping away a little bureaucracy here or divesting a business there. It meant taking a realistic look at one's company, and then deciding to reshape the place.

At the core of this decision was the assumption that it was proper, indeed, obligatory, to tamper with one's company.

Deciding to radically alter your company is easier than actually doing it.

To contemplate such an action in the early 1990s is far easier than it was a decade earlier. This is, in large measure, because Jack Welch pioneered the whole notion of restructuring. For him, however, it was most difficult.

In October 1981, six months after taking over as CEO, he spoke to 120 corporate officers. He spelled out his agenda. He wanted to begin a revolution.

There would be no more bureaucratic waste. Plans and budgets would no longer be deceptive. Difficult decisions would be made, not deferred.

> *Our issue is* **facing reality** *about having a troubled business situation. We (senior managers) can take good news and we can take bad news. We're big people and we've been paid well, all of us.*

There it is. The one business idea that ran through each and every thought espoused by Jack Welch:

FACE REALITY!

What Welch was saying was this:

Forget about the excuses. Forget about the hundred and one reasons why you failed and someone else succeeded. Forget about arguing that life is unfair, stop creating the impression that there's a conspiracy out there trying to get you.

Try to deal with situations as they are. As Welch argues:

> *The art of managing and leading comes down to a simple thing. Determining and facing REALITY about people, situations, products, and then acting decisively and quickly on that reality.*
>
> *Think how many times we have procrastinated, hoped it would get better. Most of the mistakes you have made have been through not being willing to face into it, straight in the mirror the reality you find, then taking action right on it. THAT'S ALL MANAGING IS. DEFINING AND ACTING. Not hoping, not waiting for the next plan. Not rethinking it. Getting on with it. Doing it.* Defining and doing it.

At first, it was hard for his listeners to understand all this talk of crisis.

At the end of his first year as CEO, Jack Welch addressed a group of Wall Street security analysts at the Pierre Hotel in New York. He explained—for the first time in public—what he was trying to do at General Electric:

> *If I could, this would be the appropriate moment for me to withdraw from my pocket a sealed envelope*

containing the grand strategy for the General Electric company over the next decade. But I can't, and I am not going to attempt, for the sake of intellectual neatness, to tie a bow around the many diverse initiatives of General Electric. It just doesn't make sense for neatness' sake to shoehorn these plans into an all-inclusive strategy.

What will enhance the many decentralized plans and initiatives of this company isn't a central strategy, but a central idea—a simple core concept that will guide General Electric in the 80s and govern our diverse plans and strategies.

Rather than directing GE's businesses according to a specific, step-by-step strategic plan, Welch preferred setting out only **a few clear, general goals**. Then his employees were free—but obligated—to exploit any opportunities that came their way.

Welch spelled out this strategy by citing a letter to the editor of *Fortune* magazine. The writer, Kevin Peppard, director of business development at Bendix Heavy Vehicle Systems in Elyria, Ohio, captured Welch's thinking about strategic planning for a company like GE.

Peppard observed that **Karl von Clausewitz**, the 19th century Prussian general and military historian, had written in his classic *On War*, published in 1833, that men could not reduce strategy to a formula because chance events, imperfections in execution, and the independent will of opponents automatically doomed detailed planning.

Peppard suggested that the Prussian general staff under the elder **Helmuth von Moltke**, who had been triumphant over Denmark, Austria, and France in the 1860s and early 1870s, perfected Clausewitz's concepts in practice.

They did not expect a plan of operation to survive beyond the first contact with the enemy. They set only the broadest of objectives and emphasized seizing unforeseen opportunities as they arose ... STRATEGY WAS NOT A LENGTHY ACTION PLAN. IT WAS THE EVOLUTION OF A CENTRAL IDEA THROUGH CONTINUALLY CHANGING CIRCUMSTANCES.

Welch noted that in running General Electric, he planned to adopt the same notion: **Strategy had to evolve** and not be etched in stone.

Take a moment and think about this particular business approach. At first, it may not be easy to fathom. What Welch is saying to you, the business leader of the early 1990s, is this:

You want to succeed in business?

OK, fine.

So do we all.

But don't expect me to be able to tell you how to lay out a roadmap for you.

However, it's not all that complicated.

Don't get bogged down in details.

Lay out your goals, and make sure the people who work for you pursue those goals.

And one more thing.

Face reality!

Don't pretend that all is OK when it's not. Don't assume that things will get better because time will heal what's wrong. Don't stick your head in the sand.

8

BE NUMBER ONE OR NUMBER TWO!

*"T*he winners in this slow-growth environment will be those who search out and participate in the real growth industries and insist upon being **number one or number two** in every business they are in . . ."

Gradually Jack Welch evolved a game plan, a business strategy. He called this strategy **"number one, number two."** The phrase became so familiar around General Electric that it seemed like one word, not four.

Soon after taking over as CEO, Welch became convinced that inflation would become the major enemy of American business in the 1980s.

It would lead, he said, to slower worldwide growth.

> *There will be no room for the mediocre supplier of products and services—the company in the middle of the pack.*
>
> *The winners in this slow-growth environment will be those who search out and participate in the real growth industries and insist upon being* number one or number two *in every business they are in—the* number one or number two *leanest, lowest-cost, worldwide producers of quality goods and services or those who have a clear technological edge, a clear advantage in a market niche.*

What happens when a business is far from being a leading force in the market? Here is **Jack Welch's answer.**

> *Where we are not* number one or number two, *and don't have or can't see a route to a technological edge, we have got to ask ourselves (management theorist) Peter Drucker's very tough question:*
>
> **"If you weren't already in the business, would you enter it today?"**
>
> *And if the answer is no, face into that second difficult question:*
>
> **"What are you going to do about it?"**
>
> *The managements and companies in the 80s that don't do this, that hang on to losers for whatever reason—*

> *tradition, sentiment, their own management weakness—won't be around in 1990.*
>
> *Think about the fact that in the high-growth period between 1945 and 1970, almost one-half the companies that would have been on a Fortune 500 roster disappeared either through acquisition, failure, or slipped quietly off the list due to lack of growth.*
>
> *We believe this central idea—being* **number one or number two**—*more than an objective—a requirement— will give us a set of businesses which will be unique in the world business equation at the end of the decade.*

Given the new competitiveness of the business environment, being **number one or number two** meant GE had to own and nurture only businesses that would be, in one of Jack Welch's favorite words, **"winners."**

Winning meant turning in large profits.

No longer would General Electric be able to afford the luxury of holding on to businesses that were sometimes profitable, sometimes not.

After World War II the boom periods of the 50s and 60s allowed a company like GE to coast through the ups and downs that affected some businesses, but not others.

The 80s and 90s, thanks to mounting competition from overseas, had no minor squalls, only hurricanes that left widespread devastation in their path and had the frightening prospect of bringing all businesses down at once.

Welch's business strategy was unusual. He believed a business should dominate its market. And he believed large corporations should make sure all of their businesses were dominating their markets.

Welch presided over a large, diversified portfolio of businesses—350 in all, clustered in 43 strategic business units. Few American corporations could boast such a large portfolio of businesses. And those that could were not as strong as GE across the board.

In a nutshell, this was what Jack Welch was saying:

"LET'S COMPETE ONLY IN BUSINESSES THAT WE HAVE A CHANCE TO TOWER OVER."

The business leader of the early 1990s asks quite rightly:

WHAT IF I CAN'T DEVELOP ONE OF MY BUSINESSES SO THAT IT DOMINATES A MARKET?

That is a very legitimate question. But it's not a question that Jack Welch wants you to ask. He wants you to turn the question around:

WHAT CAN I DO TO MAKE ONE OF MY BUSINESSES DOMINANT IN ITS MARKET?

Strive for excellence, Welch is saying. Make tough decisions—about which businesses are worth nurturing, which are not. Outsmart the competition. Try to determine what your opponents are doing this very minute.

It does not matter whether your corporation is huge. Most corporations are smaller than GE. But that does not matter. It is not size that is crucial. It's creating a vision and making sure everyone working with you shares that vision.

Do that, Jack Welch would say, and you're on your way to corralling the market.

Let's not have illusions. None of this is an easy sell.

It was not an easy sell for Jack Welch. The GE veterans in the early 1980s had a natural disdain for the Welch vision of keeping only the best businesses, discarding the others. Welch had no time for their disdain. He was intent upon changing the rules of the game.

Within the GE family, **performance would be the new criterion.**

Welch felt he had no choice, even though the decisions would be anguishing.

But the elephant had to become a gazelle. **The fat had to come out**.

The company had to be reshaped. It had to be put on a major diet. All this was bound to make Welch unpopular, and he knew that.

The object of suspicious, fearful employees, Jack Welch still pursued his vision. Some snickered that he was out of his mind, that he wanted to move too fast, that he did not need to restructure the company at all. Others thought little of his candor, of his profanity, and of his irreverent dismissal of GE's past.

If Welch learned of any of these rebukes, he did not let them stand in his way. He was determined to send a new message to Wall Street:

- General Electric was not some messy conglomerate with all sorts of scattered and unrelated businesses.

- The company was filled with purpose and had a focus.

- If Welch's vision was implemented quickly, General Electric would make significant progress toward its goal of being **the most competitive enterprise in the world**.

Talk about being number one or number two in a market might sound impressive, but was GE truly ready to shed some of its mature, old-line businesses that were no longer faring that well?

And what of Welch's dream to turn the company entrepreneurial? How would he overcome the inertia its history and tradition had encouraged?

Welch had answers to all these questions. But he had to convince Wall Street he was changing the nature of the lumbering, gigantic GE.

The company did not seem to be centrally focused.

It was producing such diverse products as nuclear reactors and microwave ovens, robots and silicon chips. It was involved in time-sharing services and Australian coking coal.

On the one hand, so much diversity made excelling in every field nearly impossible.

On the other hand, that same diversity gave General Electric earnings protection from economic downturns. GE had recorded 26 quarters of earnings increases in the midst of several recessions.

Still, investors had trouble understanding what General Electric produced—and how it would do in the future.

Jack Welch was determined to do something about that.

9

DOWNSIZE, BEFORE IT'S TOO LATE!

10

IN DECIDING HOW TO CHANGE YOUR BUSINESS, NOTHING SHOULD BE SACRED!

11

WHEN SEEKING THE RIGHT MARKETPLACE, THERE'S NO VIRTUE IN LOOKING FOR A FIGHT. IF YOU'RE IN A FIGHT, YOUR JOB IS TO WIN. BUT IF YOU CAN'T WIN, YOU'VE GOT TO FIND A WAY OUT.

FROM THE FILES OF *Jack Welch*

*"T*hese are the businesses that we really want to nourish. These are the businesses that will take us into the 21st century. They are **inside the circles**. **Outside the circles** you have businesses that we would prefer not to pursue any further."

Welch knew he had no choice. He knew the decisions he would make would be heart-wrenching. But the new GE had to be sleek and aggressive.

To accomplish that Welch understood he not only had to reshape the company, but he also had to reduce its size drastically.

In the early 1980s, Welch was alone in what he was doing among American business leaders—**downsizing** a company that was not in crisis.

THE WORD SOUNDED NASTY.

DOWNSIZING

The word meant pain and suffering.

It meant the loss of jobs, the loss of incomes.

This was all new terrain. The conventional wisdom had been that dismissing people should be only the last resort of a company that had already suffered serious financial reversals.

Downsizing, for that reason, had always carried the stigma of defeat, of throwing in the towel.

Because it signaled both a serious decline in the company's fortunes and an evasion of social responsibility, downsizing was to be avoided if possible.

Firing people had not been easy in the 60s and 70s. The worker enjoyed many protections.

One principle the labor unions had etched into the soul of America in the 20th century was the right of every individual to hold a job.

It was a powerful proposition. You had a right to work. You had a right not to be fired.

Politicians in Washington believed a person's work was more important than a corporation's bottom line; so they lobbied hard to preserve jobs back home.

The prevailing view among corporate managers was that a sense of job security made a worker more productive.

Yet Jack Welch believed that keeping the worker in place had become a **failed strategy**.

Keeping these workers around

COST GE HUGE AMOUNTS OF MONEY.

What was to be done?

General Electric's main competition now came from overseas companies whose workers were achieving higher productivity rates.

To match those productivity rates and hopefully surpass them—and remain competitive—GE needed to rationalize its businesses through the upgrading of equipment —and the slimming down of employee rolls.

No longer was it possible to guarantee a worker a job for life!

None of this would be easy. For one thing, the other giants on the American corporate scene did not share Welch's view of the modern corporation. No other chief executive was prepared to perform radical surgery on his own company as Welch was. No other chief executive was going to rush to Jack Welch's defense.

The effect of Welch's downsizing would be to put thousands of General Electric employees out of work. Inevitably, Jack Welch became targeted for acting with excessive cruelty toward the worker.

He was persuaded, however, that only through this **massive surgery** would GE improve.

He did not ask: Is the **revolution** worth the pain and suffering I am inflicting on these people?

He did not ask whether he owed these people continuing job security. These were not options for Jack Welch. His job was not to make people happy. It was to **make the company as profitable as possible**.

Jack Welch's **revolution** formed around a new principle:

NOTHING WAS SACRED.

In the past nearly everything and everyone at General Electric had been homegrown. From the very beginning down through World War II, General Electric had developed and built its own businesses for the most part.

That had always been considered one of GE's great strengths. After more than 100 years of accomplishment came enormous pride.

The pride, however, nurtured a kind of do-it-yourself culture. Nearly everyone had joined the firm at an early age and risen through the ranks. They talked mostly to other GE employees. They learned to bristle at anything "not invented here."

But now the company had to **stop looking inward**.

It had to step out into the new world.

That meant **shedding businesses and managers and employees who were not producing**.

It meant **bringing in new businesses and new managers and new employees who could produce**.

This was the essence of this bold, new strategy called

RESTRUCTURING.

Within GE at first there was sheer disbelief.

The questions came fast and furious:

Why was it necessary to be number one or two?

What was wrong with being a good number three or four?

What if we discard a business that is not number one or two now, but in another decade might become a great winner?

Again, Jack Welch had answers. He told the cynics: In many cyclical businesses it was precisely the number three, four, five, or six business that got hurt during a cyclical downturn.

Number one or two businesses were not going to lose market share.

- Because they had a leadership position, they could employ more aggressive pricing.

- Because of that position, they had the resources to bring out new products.

Often, the leaders of businesses who thought they were third or fourth had been ranking themselves only against domestic competition and were in fact seventh or eighth.

Welch digs into his own experience to explain the difference between a number one or two company and one that is not as strong:

> *I ran some businesses that were number one or two and some businesses that were four or five so I had the luxury of a laboratory . . . So I had some that were leaders and some were big followers. And it was clear to me that one (the number one) was a helluva lot easier and better than the other one (the weaker businesses). The other one didn't have the resources and the muscle and the power to compete on a global scale that was emerging in the 90s.*

Some had glimmerings of doubt about the "number one, number two" approach. They felt that Welch, using his yardstick, just might sweep away a business that in another decade could be a great winner.

This point was made by Mark Markovitz, an engineer with GE in Schenectady, who, in a letter to the editor in *Fortune*, wrote:

> *Jack Welch's predecessors—Ralph Cordiner, Fred Borch, and Reginald Jones—nurtured the Aircraft Engine, Gas Turbine, and Plastics businesses when they were small or money-losing operations. What chance of survival would they have had under Mr. Welch's No. 1 or No. 2 test?*

None of this perturbed Jack Welch. Early in 1982 he took a pad and pencil and sketched

THREE CIRCLES.

> *These are the businesses that we really want to nourish. These are the businesses that will take us into the 21st century. They are inside the circles. Outside the circles you have businesses that we would prefer not to pursue any further.*

One circle contained GE's **core businesses**; the second circle, GE's **high-technology businesses**; the third circle, GE's **service businesses**.

The businesses inside these circles would receive the company's resources. Those outside would not. Welch's vision had become more concrete, more focused.

Anyone who wanted to know what General Electric was all about could simply look at the circles, look at which businesses were inside and which were not.

Fifteen businesses went into those circles. These were the businesses that Jack Welch deemed to have the best chance to be big winners in their fields through the 1980s and into the early 1990s. When taken together, these units produced 90 percent of corporate earnings in 1984.

Being placed outside the circle did not automatically mean a permanent stay in purgatory.

In fact, Welch adopted a motto.

"FIX, CLOSE, OR SELL."

That became the company's strategy for dealing with businesses outside the circles. If it was possible to fix a business and bring it back inside the circles, that was fine.

But the chances were that GE would sell the business to someone who liked that business more than General Electric did. Jack Welch explained the purpose of the three circles:

> *Some people say I'm afraid to compete. I think one of the jobs of a businessperson is to get away from slug-fests and into niches where you can prevail.* **The fundamental goal is to get rid of weakness, to find a sheltered womb where no one can hurt you.** *There's no virtue in looking for a fight. If you're in a fight, your job is to win. But if you can't win, you've got to find a way out.*

The **three circles concept** was Jack Welch's compass as he navigated through the early 1980s. He used the concept as a framework for bringing clarity to an organization that outside cynics had dubbed nothing more than a messy conglomerate.

How did Jack Welch decide which businesses were placed inside or outside the circle?

I'm looking at the competitive arena. Where does the business sit?

What are its **strengths** *vis-à-vis the competition?*

And what are its **weaknesses?**

What can the competition do to us despite our hard work that can kill us a year or two years down the road?

What can we do to them to change the playing field?

In a business you lay out the world competitive arena, the market size, the players in each pool, the global share, so you get the playing field defined. Then you ask somebody:

What have you done in the last two years to improve your relative position in that?

What moves have you made? What moves has the competition made in the last two years to change the playing field in its favor?

What dynamite move could you make in the next two years to change the playing field in your favor, and what are you most frightened about that (the competition) might do to change your game?

That's all you really need. If you have a game that's vulnerable, somebody can move fast, get you. And you don't have a checkmate play or another move. You've got to get out of that game.

Welch's **three circles** sent shivers through the organization.

Inside the services circle were the following GE businesses:

General Electric Credit Corporation.

Information.

Construction and Engineering.

Nuclear Services.

Inside the technology circle were:

Industrial Electronics.

Medical Systems.

Materials.

Aerospace.

Aircraft Engines.

Inside the core circle were:

Lighting.

Major Appliance.

Motor.

Transportation.

Turbine.

Contractor Equipment.

Outside the circle were these GE businesses:

Housewares.

Central Air Conditioning.

TV & Audio.

Cable.

Mobile Communications.

Power Delivery.

Radio Stations.

Ladd Petroleum.

Semiconductor.

Trading.

Utah International.

Calma.

Very few of these businesses are part of GE today.

The three circles idea was Jack Welch's way of defending GE against those who dismissed GE as a mere conglomerate.

Those lucky enough to be inside the circles liked the security of being there. But those relegated to the purgatory outside the circles were distinctly uncomfortable.

Those outside the circle felt that Jack Welch had sent them a clear message: that he had placed them outside the circles not to encourage them to work harder in order to get inside, but because he intended to put their businesses up for sale.

This strategy—the **number one, number two** strategy—can work only if the company adopts what Jack Welch calls

SOFT VALUES.

What are these soft values?

REALITY
QUALITY/EXCELLENCE
THE HUMAN ELEMENT

Reality means General Electric employees had, in Welch's words, "to see the world the way it is and not the way they wished it were or hoped it would be."

Quality and excellence meant "stretching beyond our limits, to be, in some cases, better than we ever thought we could be."

The human element meant that people dared "to try new things."

Follow these values, Jack Welch argued, and the company would become more

HIGH-SPIRITED,
ADAPTABLE,
AGILE.

Those were the values he was seeking to make General Electric run more smoothly than enterprises far smaller.

Reaction to Welch's first efforts at restructuring were strident. He was given the nickname "Neutron Jack"—an allusion to the neutron bomb that eliminates people but leaves the buildings standing. He hated the name and thought it most unfair because it indicated he had been unfair to his employees.

That nickname haunted Jack Welch. It was used to define him in the media as a heartless soul caring only for the bottom line and not for the welfare of his employees.

Welch was always embittered at the phrase.

"I think it was a harsh term," he said softly, but with anger apparent in his voice. "Mean-spirited. They call me 'Neutron Jack' because we laid off people even though we gave them the best benefits they had in their life."

Welch felt deep inside that he was a caring person, but one with the insight to understand that the only way to build a company in these perilous times was not to turn General Electric into a welfare society but to create a solid, lean, agile company.

The welfare society would eventually stagnate. The lean and agile GE had a chance to make it.

Welch's leadership secrets on downsizing and the three circles apply to all business leaders trying to figure out how to turn their businesses around.

Welch is saying:

- Take a good, hard look at your business and don't be afraid to make some major decisions on how to get your costs down.

- Decide which of your employees and your businesses you truly need, which you do not.

- And then, don't get emotionally involved in the consequences of your decisions, however painful they are going to be.

- Don't dither. The quicker you make these decisions, the better off you and your business will be.

12

CREATE A CULTURE, THEN SPREAD IT!

FROM THE FILES OF Jack Welch

"I really want to use Crotonville and this Crotonville process to have a **cultural revolution** in this company."

From the beginning, Jack Welch understood that it was not enough to craft a business philosophy. It was crucial to get his ideas to the widest possible audience at General Electric. It was not enough to start a revolution.

Every General Electric employee, or at least as many as possible, had to be brought on board—and as quickly as possible.

This is a valuable lesson for the business leader of the 1990s. Brilliant business ideas are good. Brilliant speeches are good. But ideas and speeches are not enough. You've got to be certain that you are getting your message across.

For Jack Welch, the way to do it was through the sprawling campus that was General Electric's Management Development Institute at Crotonville, New York. For you—today's business leader—it will be other Crotonville-like experiences. Let's look briefly at what Jack Welch did.

When Welch became chief executive officer, he could have closed Crotonville. He could have concluded it was too costly. He could have accused it of serving the irrelevancies of the past.

Rather, he decided to keep it open—and use it to further his own objectives. He saw in the place the same potential for transmitting the CEO's message that his predecessors had seen.

He was saving money in other parts of the company, but not at Crotonville. There, he spent $45 million on new buildings and other improvements.

Some protested.

Welch ignored the critics. He wanted to make GE more productive, and leaner.

One of the best ways of doing that, he believed, was to make sure the management training program existed and was used to foster his goals for the company.

Fortune magazine called Crotonville **"the Harvard of corporate America."** The place does look like a college campus.

Crotonville began in early 1956, the brainchild of Ralph Cordiner, General Electric's chairman and chief executive officer in the 1950s. It was created as a command and general staff school to disseminate the virtues of decentralization, the central business strategy of GE at the time.

Later, Fred Borch and Reginald Jones, Cordiner's first two successors, used Crotonville as an indoctrination center—to disseminate the notion of strategic planning.

The original textbooks written for the Crotonville seminars became legendary in the business world. The founding "professors" at Crotonville wrote eight volumes on professional management. The volumes were known simply as **"The Blue Books."**

As Jack Welch said soon after taking over:

> *I really want to use Crotonville and the Crotonville process to have a* **cultural revolution** *in this company.*

Poring through the 154-page curriculum and gazing at the courses offered, one might think that Crotonville is nothing more than a business school.

It offers courses in:

The new manager.

The experienced manager.

Advanced financial management.

Advanced information technology management.

Advanced marketing management.

Applied creative thinking and interpersonal communications.

It is not, however, just another business school.

It is the place where Jack Welch's philosophy percolates through the GE layers. It is where senior executives, Jack Welch among them, learn what is taking place in the company.

Walter Wriston, the former Citicorp chairman and a member of the GE board, once told Welch:

> *Jack, remember one thing, you're always going to be the last one to know the critical things that need to be done in your organization. Everyone else already knows.*

Jack Welch uses Crotonville to make sure he is not the last one to find out what is going on at General Electric.

Welch visits Crotonville at least once a month to lecture and answer questions. He enjoys the combative atmosphere that prevails at Crotonville, especially in

THE PIT.

All of Crotonville's objectives come together in the Pit, which is a large lecture hall with elevated seats that force the lecturer to look up at the audience. Hence, the lecturer feels as if he or she were at the bottom of a pit.

In one strange way the name and the surroundings encourage give-and-take.

It is in the Pit that GE executives speak their minds, argue, dissent, take on Jack Welch and other senior GE executives.

It is in the Pit that Jack Welch seems most in his element, tossing around the grand ideas, arguing with GE employees.

It is his best chance to win over employees to his point of view. It is a golden opportunity for him to learn what troubles the people at GE.

The aim of the dialogue that goes on in the Pit is the opposite of blind obedience. People must have the self-confidence to express contrasting views. They get it in part because they are looking down at the speaker, and the speaker is looking up at them.

One of the most effective weapons in Welch's arsenal is

CANDOR.

He employs it at Crotonville. To make sure that nothing leaks out and that participants feel free to be candid, he bars journalists, security analysts, and consultants (though the author was made an exception and offered a glimpse of the place).

To acquire feedback, each participant is expected to fill in a one-page appraisal sheet and answer three questions:

- What did you find about the presentation that was constructive and clarifying?

- What did you find confusing or troublesome?

- What do you regard as your most important take-away from this session?

Crotonville is not restricted to a single location. It is a process. Managers engage in Crotonville-driven exercises around the world.

Here is Jim Baughman, the man in charge of Crotonville, talking about that process:

> *Sometimes it's a platform, sometimes a listening post, sometimes a debating mechanism, sometimes a pulpit, sometimes a crying towel ... That process gives*

all the members of the CEO—not just Jack—a way on any given day to track the company.

The number one thing we're trying to achieve is to create and nourish a high-performing team. That's what leadership is. It isn't someone on a horse commanding the troops. It's the ability to . . . create a vision, to have a high-performing team around that vision. The high-performing team is the key organizational ingredient in GE today.

Business leaders need a place like Crotonville. One could dispense with the sprawling campus, the marvelous recreational facilities, and the other parts of Crotonville that make it so physically attractive.

However, if you are going to get your message across to large segments of the business, some means must be found to communicate easily, quickly, and to large numbers of your employees.

It is important to have a vision. It is just as important to be able to communicate that vision to others.

That is the leadership secret embodied in the Crotonville idea.

13

DON'T GET STUCK IN THE PAST!
BE OPEN TO CHANGE!

14

REEXAMINE YOUR AGENDA CONSTANTLY
AND, IF NECESSARY, REWRITE IT!

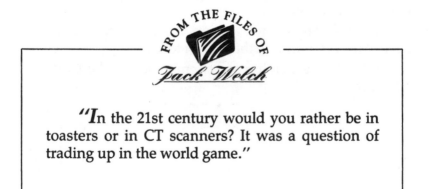

*"I*n the 21st century would you rather be in toasters or in CT scanners? It was a question of trading up in the world game."

Managing, to Jack Welch, is a term of the past. And he does not like the past!

A manager, as far as he is concerned, has

TO LEAD

not simply manage.

Welch prefers not to use the term *manager*. He prefers

BUSINESS LEADER.

For Jack Welch, tradition is always irrelevant. He hates the past, with its habits and attitudes that have no meaning for the present.

GE was in the hands of someone who did not want to be chained to the company's tradition. He was insensitive to its vaunted history.

In short, Welch did not want the company to live on its laurels.

FOR HIM, THE PAST WAS OVER.

You can't do anything about it. Right or wrong, good or bad. You learn from it, but I mean it can't do much for me. I'm a person who lives in tomorrow, though, and tries like hell to get out of yesterday.

What had been suitable for General Electric in the past was not automatically right for it now. What would make or break Welch's career, he knew, was not whether he paid enough attention to the company's traditions, but whether he could shape the company and the people who worked for it in new ways.

Molding people was as important as molding the company. For instance, in the old days at GE, managers worked with what they were given, with what they had. The old way at the company was to "memo" a problem to death.

The idea had been to conduct meetings on a problem until the problem went away or was overwhelmed by another problem.

JACK WELCH HAD A DIFFERENT WAY.

His way was to treat the company as an arena of competition in the same way that a hockey rink or golf course was. He played to win in sports. It was the same for him in business.

It seemed only fitting that the man who had dedicated himself to the task of creating the most competitive enterprise on earth had to be competitive himself.

To carry out that mission he had to be tough-minded as well.

For Welch, one way to avoid falling back on old habits was to be certain General Electric was always open to change.

He had unleashed a revolution at GE. But it would do the company no good to move from old patterns to the Welch way—and then freeze in another inflexible pattern.

Instead, Jack Welch argued:

YOU'VE GOT TO REEXAMINE YOUR AGENDA CONSTANTLY AND, IF NECESSARY, REWRITE IT!

Yes, even his own precepts could be cast aside if demonstrated to be wrong. He wanted managers to come to work and occasionally act as if they were **new on the job**—and to think hard about what could be changed for the better.

No greater example exists of Welch's willingness to forget the past and concentrate on the future than his selling of GE's household appliances business in 1983.

The sale of that GE business proved the most anguishing divestiture for General Electric employees.

But that did not deter Jack Welch.

Giving up on toasters and irons and fans, the disgruntled critics insisted, was selling off the company's heritage. These were the items that had made the company a household name across the land.

The business had been deemed an essential part of GE's portfolio because anytime a housewife bought a toaster or a coffeepot or a steam iron, the company's public exposure was enhanced.

GE had had substantial, profitable positions in lighting and major appliances, and as Reg Jones, the former CEO at General Electric, noted:

> *I'd always felt we needed housewares to fill the gap between the two so that Mrs. Consumer could go into a retail establishment and see the General Electric line.*

Had the business been wonderfully profitable, its more unpleasant aspects might have been overlooked. But, being a scrawny financial performer, the heartaches stood out.

Paul Van Orden, who ran the housewares business in the late 1970s, recalled what a source of consumer complaints the business was:

> *Blankets burnt, mixers broke down, coffee makers caught on fire. The toaster oven is an abomination. It's an oxymoron. It doesn't toast very well; it doesn't broil. You can't get the meat brown.*

Welch's decision to sell the housewares business was not universally welcome, but he was surprised at the negative reaction.

Housewares had been a mainstream GE business in the past.

Crotonville's Jim Baughman recalled the controversy:

> *People said how can you exit housewares? How can you do that? It's a GE tradition. Welch's answer was: "In the 21st century would you rather be in toasters or in CT scanners? It was a question of trading up in the world game."*

Housewares had been good for the GE of the past. It had no part in the GE of the future as Joyce Hergenhan, vice president for public relations, noted:

> *Our strengths were lost in a business like housewares. You come up with some great new hair dryer, let's say, and within two months, all over the Middle East people would be coming up with a lower-priced knockoff of the same thing. GE's strengths are technology, its technological resources, its financial resources, and a business like housewares didn't play to those strengths at all.*

Reg Jones and Jack Welch got into a small wrangle when the current CEO asked his predecessor what he thought of the idea of selling the housewares business.

Jones suggested that GE's franchise with the consumer could be harmed and would in turn damage the lighting and major appliance businesses.

Welch quoted from a marketing survey he had initiated that suggested shoppers would go on purchasing GE's lamps and appliances even after it no longer sold housewares.

As it turned out, Welch was right: Exiting housewares had no impact on other GE businesses.

In this case, being number one or two in the market was not enough. Housewares had achieved dominance in its markets. Yet it had a major drawback in Welch's eyes: It was not a business with great growth potential.

It was a business living in the past. It was a business steeped in General Electric tradition.

But it was not performing effectively.

You know what Jack Welch would say.

Reexamine your agenda. Housewares was part of an old agenda. So rewrite the agenda. Drop housewares.

All of us must have a "housewares" lurking in our midst, a piece of the corporation that everyone loves, everyone is used to, that everyone thinks must be left alone.

But ask yourself—why be so wedded to the past?

We can hear you now.

It's easier, you say. It's harder to change.

Sure, it's harder to change. But keep thinking of Jack Welch's leadership secret 13: Don't get stuck in the past. Be open to change!

It's a leadership secret that can only help.

Keep it in mind as we look at Jack Welch's business ideas in greater depth.

15

TRANSFER IDEAS AND ALLOCATE RESOURCES AND THEN GET OUT OF THE WAY.

16

MAKE SURE EVERYONE IN YOUR BUSINESS GETS ALL THE INFORMATION REQUIRED TO MAKE DECISIONS.

17

PROVIDE AN ATMOSPHERE WHERE PEOPLE CAN HAVE THE RESOURCES TO GROW, THE EDUCATIONAL TOOLS ARE AVAILABLE, AND THEY CAN EXPAND THEIR HORIZONS.

*"P*eople always overestimate how complex business is. This isn't rocket science. **We've chosen one of the world's most simple professions.**"

Jack Welch's theories on management start with the following premise:

BUSINESS IS SIMPLE!

Business is very simple. **People who try to make it complex get themselves all wound around.**

People always overestimate how complex business is. This isn't rocket science. **We've chosen one of the world's most simple professions.** *Most global businesses have three or four critical competitors, and you know who they are.* **And there aren't that many things you can do with a business.** *It's not as if you're choosing among 2,000 options.*

I operate on a very simple belief about business. If there are six of us in a room and we all get the same facts, in most cases the six of us will all reach roughly the same conclusion. The problem is, we don't get the same information. We each get different pieces. **Business isn't complicated.** *The complications arise when people are cut off from information they need.*

A good manager, keeping business simple, needs to ask only five questions in order to make clear, speedy decisions. However, they must be

THE RIGHT FIVE QUESTIONS.

They are:

- What does your global competitive environment look like?

- In the last three years, what have your competitors done?

- In the same period, what have you done to them?

- How might they attack you in the future?

- What are your plans to leapfrog them?

Because he regards business as essentially a knowable science, Welch is not put off by dealing with large enterprises. In fact, the bigger, the better.

He enjoys presiding over General Electric because it is the most complex, the most diverse.

Still, it seems unbelievable that one man could run 13 major businesses. How did Welch keep up with each of them?

> *There are a series of mechanisms that allow you to keep in touch. I travel around the world often, so I'm smelling what people are thinking. I'm at Crotonville. I get feedback sheets. I have CEC (Corporate Executive Council) meetings where GE's business leaders come in for two days and talk about the businesses. None of us runs the businesses. I'm never going to run them. I don't run them at all. If I tried to run them, I'd go crazy.* **I can smell when someone running (a business) isn't doing it right.**

It would be incorrect to think of Jack Welch as a manager in the normal sense of the word.

Welch is more of a

SUPERMANAGER,

overseeing 13 businesses all at once.

> *"My job," he says by way of summing up the task of running this mammoth enterprise, "is to put the best people on the biggest opportunities and the best allocation of dollars in the right places. That's about it.*

Transfer ideas and allocate resources and get out of the way."

But because Jack Welch has been so successful at managing, his views on what it takes to be a good manager have been listened to attentively.

This was somewhat paradoxical—for Welch believes

A GOOD MANAGER IS SOMEONE WHO ALL BUT GIVES UP MANAGING!

With far fewer employees after downsizing, those employees remaining would have to do only the most important tasks.

This was a positive development to Jack Welch.

> *(Our employees will) have to set priorities. The less important tasks have to be left undone. Trying to do the same number of tasks with fewer people would be the antithesis of what we set out to achieve:*
>
> A faster, more focused, more purposeful company.
>
> *As we became leaner, we found ourselves communicating better, with fewer interpreters and fewer filters. We found that with fewer layers we had wider spans of management.*
>
> We weren't managing better. We were managing less, and that was better.

There it was—the nub of Jack Welch's business philosophy:

MANAGING LESS IS MANAGING BETTER

> *It's sometimes dangerous to call somebody a manager.*

> *For the term* manager, *Welch says, had come to mean someone who "controls rather than facilitates, complicates rather than simplifies, acts more like a governor than an accelerator."*

Welch liked to distinguish between leaders and managers.

> Leaders—*and you take anyone from Roosevelt to Churchill to Reagan—inspire people with* clear visions *of how things can be done better. Some managers, on the other hand, muddle things with pointless complexity and detail. They equate (managing) with sophistication, with sounding smarter than anyone else. They inspire no one. I dislike the traits that have come to be associated with "managing"—controlling, stifling people, keeping them in the dark, wasting their time on trivia and reports. Breathing down their necks. You can't manage self-confidence into people.*

YOU HAVE TO GET OUT OF THEIR WAY AND LET IT GROW IN THEM BY ALLOWING THEM TO WIN, AND THEN REWARDING THEM WHEN THEY DO.

In the summer of 1992 Jack Welch described his own job as supermanager of GE:

> *My job is:* resource allocation, dollars, and ideas. *That's all I do. And my job is to be sure I bet on the right people, that I give the right businesses the right amount of money and that I transfer ideas rapidly from business A to B. (My job) is not to know if that compressor should (act this way or that). It's to challenge good people with the right questions: Should we make it ourselves? Should we buy it from the Italians? What will be the*

implications five years from now of making or buying it? What do we bring to the party by making it? What is added value? Then get out of town. If it's $25 million or less, ask no questions (how the money is spent). (We) delegate it to people. Ask nothing. We take a couple of billion dollars of capital and we parcel it out to our businesses. That's the last time we see $2 billion.

The word manager has too often come to be synonymous with control—cold, uncaring, buttoned-down, passionless.

I NEVER ASSOCIATED PASSION WITH THE WORD MANAGER, AND I'VE NEVER SEEN A LEADER WITHOUT IT.

What companies and business leaders must do, says Welch,

is provide an atmosphere, a climate, a chance, a meritocracy, where people can have the resources to grow, the educational tools are available, they can expand their horizons, their vision of life. That's what companies ought to provide. If you can get an environment that's open, where people aren't going to say NO!, where they're willing to experiment with you—People say to me, "Aren't you afraid of losing control. You're not measuring (anymore)." We couldn't lose control of this place. We've got 106 years of people measuring everything. So we're not going to lose control. It's in our blood.

In a speech at Fairfield University on October 14, 1982, 18 months after he became chief executive officer at GE, Welch fired an early shot on the subject of management. He recalled that in the high-growth period of the 50s and 60s

> *There was a real need for caretakers. But in the 80s,*
> *where growth is anything but a given, we're going to*
> *need the entrepreneurs, the leaders, who won't be*
> *handed growth opportunities but who will make*
> *growth happen.*

In a period of slower growth, the best kind of business-person, according to Jack Welch, was the one

> *With the courage to take command, to run with it.*

That meant instilling greater self-confidence in General Electric's employees.

> *We're trying to give people who run our businesses a*
> *keen* sense of ownership, *so they will run them as en-*
> *trepreneurs rather than as caretakers.*

He elaborated on what it took to be a good manager in an interview he gave to GE's house organ, *Monogram*, in the fall of 1987.

> *Clearly, a manager will have to be much more com-*
> *fortable being open. The idea of the manager knowing a*
> *little bit more than his or her subordinates is over ...*
> *The manager—and maybe I like the word* leader *bet-*
> *ter—who is able to get everybody to share information,*
> *to really communicate until they all know the same*
> *thing and thus share a* common vision, *is tomorrow's*
> *manager ... The idea of the foreman, the manager,*
> *knowing a few more facts and then using those facts to*
> *become "the boss"—that's 1950s, 1960s stuff.*

Today, tomorrow, it's everybody sharing the same information at every level—from the top to the bottom. And, hopefully, top to the bottom is fewer and fewer layers every single day.

> *The mind-set of yesterday's manager was to accept compromise and keep things neat, which tended to breed complacency.* **Tomorrow's leaders, on the other hand, raise issues, debate them, resolve them.** *They aren't afraid to go against today's current because they know* **their constituency is tomorrow.** *They rally people around a vision of what a business can become.* **They rely less on controls than on trust.** *Managers and officers need to do better at one-on-one communicating with individuals—about their jobs and aspirations.*

What is Jack Welch talking about?

Is he making any sense?

What's all this advice about managing less?

Maybe Welch's business philosophy works at General Electric, so large, so complicated that maybe a little less managing wouldn't hurt, but what does this have to do with my business?

Good questions, questions that a business leader in the 1990s is bound to ask.

Let's try to figure out what Welch really means.

What he's suggesting to you—the manager of a big corporation, the middle-manager of a middle-sized company, whatever kind of manager you are—is simply this:

Stop standing in the way of the people who work for you.

They're a lot smarter than you probably are giving them credit for.

Stop looking over their shoulder. Stop bogging them down in all sorts of bureaucratic obstacles.

Show them some respect. Make them feel that what they are doing is important. And get the hell out of their way!

Now, what's so hard about that?

Very hard, you say.

After all, we, the managers of American businesses, have been trained to do just that—to manage. That has to mean managing, controlling, supervising, creating structures in the company that make sure things get done.

Fine.

Now ask yourself another question.

In today's business environment, are the things that seemed to be true, that seemed to be valid, the very things that are keeping us from getting ahead?

Look at Welch's record at GE.

He's been preaching a philosophy of managing less— and the performance of the company is spectacular.

Maybe what he says has some merit.

18

DELAYER: GET RID OF THE FAT!

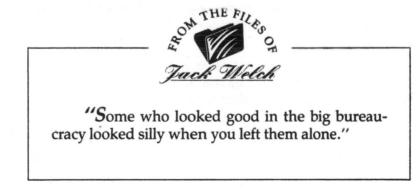

*"*S*ome who looked good in the big bureau-cracy looked silly when you left them alone."*

Here comes the difficult part.

Here comes the painful part.

Jack Welch preaches candor, he preaches reality—and now we get to that part of the story where candor and reality, if adopted as our watchwords, will push our companies forward.

But, in becoming realistic, we will find that we have to go through some unpleasant moments. So get ready for a rough ride. In the end, you will decide whether it was worth it.

Jack Welch had no trouble deciding the pain and suffering were worth it. He began by peeling away the layers of fat at General Electric.

He was convinced that the only way to liberate everyone—from the top managers to the folks on the factory floor—was to rid the company of its excess baggage.

Accordingly, layers of management had to be eradicated. In the old days, those layers had been considered beneficial. It was hard to recall why.

Jack Welch snubbed his nose at GE's former strategic planning technique that was characterized by all those layers. The technique, he insisted, was not supple, it slowed things down, and it did not help managers spot trouble quickly enough.

The emphasis on strategic planning and control and formality had cultivated a climate that sapped the kind of entrepreneurial spirit a large company like General Electric needed.

It was that stifling of the entrepreneurial spirit that bothered Jack Welch more than anything else.

The original idea of the strategic planning process and the new bureaucracy that had come in its wake had appeared sound. Bureaucracy was not a dirty word.

"In fact," according to Gertrude Michelson, a GE board member since 1976, "in a way it represented organization, orderliness. You had a boss, and he had a boss, and somebody else had a boss, and you went through channels, you wrote memos, that was the way an orderly business was run."

Yet General Electric had grown so immense and so diverse that it seemed nearly everyone was a manager of some sort. Of its 400,000 employees, 25,000 had the title of "manager." Some 500 were senior managers, and 130 were vice presidents or higher. This flock of supervisors engaged in little else but reviewing what their subordinates were doing.

In theory such reviews seemed necessary to keep the enterprise moving in the right direction. In practice, however, managers wound up spending an inordinate amount of time filling out routine reports and selling their plans to other more senior managers.

When Fred Borch and Reg Jones, the two CEOs at General Electric who had preceded Welch, had reclustered the business units into 43 strategic business units, the command-and-control function was supposed to improve dramatically.

But the addition of a new layer of bureaucracy of finance and planning staffs resulted in executives commanding and controlling one another, leaving no time for determining how a business was performing.

The planning system, Jack Welch asserted, "was dynamite when we first put it in." But the format was cumbersome.

We hired a head of planning and he hired two vice presidents and then he hired a planner, and then the books got thicker, and the printing got more

> *sophisticated and the covers got harder and the draw-*
> *ings got better. The meetings kept getting larger.*
> *Nobody can say anything with 16 or 18 people there.*

The paperwork was endless.

Dennis Dammerman, senior vice president, finance, re-membered ordering the shutting down of a GE computer that had been grinding out daily reports for no apparent reason. The computer had produced a stack of paper 12 feet high.

The reports contained product-by-product sales infor-mation—down to the penny—on hundreds of thousands of items. Executives felt compelled to look through the re-ports, to analyze them, to talk about them to one another.

Little time was left for studying the big picture.

THE WHOLE SYSTEM HAD SIMPLY BECOME TOO BUREAUCRATIC.

Indeed, strategic planning had become an unhealthy force in the company, attaching more importance to style and structure than to substance.

Its most characteristic feature was the memo. Memo writing became a way of life, and managers fired them at one another with such tenacity that executives might have mistakenly concluded their main task in life was simply to read!

For all its flaws, the system did assure that nothing went terribly amiss.

But little more.

Jack Welch decided to slice away at management levels. He called the process **delayering**.

Some said that getting rid of these levels reduced GE's needed command and control and harmed the company.

Jack Welch disagreed.

*I couldn't wipe out the command-and-control sys-
tem that's inherent in this company financially. We
attempted to eliminate the command portion while
keeping the subtleties of the control. Big corporations
are filled with people in bureaucracy who want to cover
things—cover the bases, say they did everything a little
bit. Well, now we have people out there all by themselves, there they are, accountable—for their successes
and their failures. But it gives them a chance to flourish.
Now you see some wilt. That's the sad part of the job.
Some who looked good in the big bureaucracy looked
silly when you left them alone. They looked OK. They
had support. They presented themselves well, came in
with charts, didn't look anywhere near as bad as they
looked all by themselves.*

To get rid of the command portion, Welch embarked on
a methodical campaign to dismantle the layers of bureaucracy that had grown up in the 60s and 70s.

He had a dual purpose:

To turn the strategic planning function over to the
businesses.

And to remove the obstacles that prevented direct
contact among the businesses and between the business and the CEO's office.

The subtleties of control would remain. But it would be
far easier for everyone to communicate with everyone else.

Delayering is not just meant to reduce costs. It im-
proves management, according to Welch.

*We did a study that showed we saved $40 million by
removing the sectors, but that's just a fraction of the*

*real value. That doesn't account for the improved
quality of our leadership, or how fast we can get to
market now.* Delayering speeds communications. It
returns control and accountability to the businesses,
which is where it belongs.

*We got two other great benefits from the sector de-
layering. First, by taking out the biggest layer of top
management, we set a role model for the whole company about becoming* lean and agile.

*Second, we identified the business leaders who
didn't share the values we were talking about—*candor,
facing reality, lean and agile. *We exposed the passive
resisters, the ones who were right for another time but
didn't have the energy to energize others for the global
challenges ahead.*

This is indeed the hard part. It's one thing to get rid of
the employees, the folks who work on the factory floor, far
from the corporate office. It's quite another to take an ax to
a fellow manager, an associate in the corporate office, a
buddy.

Delayering, in some ways, takes the most amount of
courage on your part.

If you want to be just an ordinary manager, you'll find
Jack Welch's delayering tactics far too sensitive a business
tactic. The whole thing may seem so distasteful you don't
even want to begin.

To become a high-performance business leader, however, follow his advice. Take a hard look at all those layers
of management—and then decide.

Where can I cut?

How can I improve my communications with the folks
down below on the factory floor?

It worked for Jack Welch.

GE's management became more efficient. More important, the company's productivity rose.

Try it.

It will hurt—for a while. Jack Welch's path is not strewn with roses. But it has worked for him.

Go ahead and begin the process, a process called delayering.

19

EXPRESS A VISION, THEN LET YOUR EMPLOYEES IMPLEMENT IT ON THEIR OWN!

FROM THE FILES OF
Jack Welch

"We don't claim to be the global fountainhead of management thought, but we may be the world's thirstiest pursuer of big ideas—from whatever their source—and we're not shy about adopting and adapting them."

What is a good manager?

In Jack Welch's mind, he or she is someone

- Who does less supervising.

- Who delegates further down into the company.

- Who lets the businesses under him or her develop plans that make sense for their marketplaces.

- Who allows the people under him or her to decide how and when and where to spend large sums of money on their plant and equipment.

A **good manager** takes it as a given that the people under him or her—the lower-level managers, the foremen and forewomen, the employees themselves—have a better grasp than the manager does of what the reality of a business is. Of how the marketplace is shaping up.

A **good manager** expresses a vision and then has the good sense to let the people who work for him or her try to implement it on their own. Part of that vision concerns getting the most possible out of employees, not holding back, encouraging them to take risks.

In the early days Jack Welch had made his name by marketing products with new features that bested the competition.

Such leapfrogging was part and parcel of what he called the

"QUANTUM LEAP."

The good manager searches for such a **quantum leap,** whether it is marketing a superior product or acquiring a business that boosts market share dramatically.

Welch believes the senior manager's job is to deal with complexity.

The more responsibility a manager has, the better decisions he or she will make.

> *I think people take more responsibility for their action when they're the last signature. If you're just one of 20 signatures on a decision to buy a new thing, and you're the 17th signature, and it's got to go to three more bosses, I think your signature means less than if you're the final decider.*

Welch liked to point to the experience of Appliance Park in Louisville, Kentucky, to illustrate what empowerment could do.

For years the product had moved down the assembly line whether or not a worker was finished doing his or her job.

Welch had that system changed. The employee was given the responsibility of deciding when to move the product from his or her station to the next.

> *People on the assembly line suddenly found two levers in front of them. One lever stopped the line. The other sent a part on its way only after an individual was satisfied that it was perfect. The line workers suddenly became the final authority on the quality of their work. The cynics scoffed when this system was proposed, predicting chaos or production at a snail's pace. What happened? Quality increased enormously and the line ran faster and smoother than ever.*

This was an example of **managing less**. This was an example of empowerment.

Welch describes four types of GE managers and assesses who would succeed at GE, who would fail.

THE FIRST TYPE

delivers on commitments—financial or otherwise—and shares GE's values. "His or her future is an easy call: Onward and upward."

THE SECOND TYPE

does not meet commitments (read "bring in a healthy balance sheet") and does not share GE's values. "Not as pleasant a call but equally easy."

THE THIRD TYPE

misses commitments but shares the values. "He or she usually gets a second chance, preferably in a different environment."

THE FOURTH TYPE

delivers on commitments but does not subscribe to GE's values. This type is the most difficult to deal with.

> *This is the individual who typically forces performance out of people rather than inspires it; the autocrat, the big shot, the tyrant. Too often all of us have looked the other way—tolerated these "Type 4" managers because "they always deliver"—at least in the short term.*
>
> *And perhaps this type is more acceptable in easier times, but in an environment where we must have every good idea from every man and woman in the organization, we cannot afford management styles that suppress and intimidate. Whether we can convince and help these managers to change—recognizing how difficult that can be—or part company with them if they cannot—will be the ultimate test . . ."*

If a manager does not pass on GE values, what happens to the manager?

> *Even managers and officers with good numbers (get fired). That's a shell shock to our company because numbers are no longer job security. Values and numbers now mean job security. That's a big transformation. At Work-Out (GE's new program that encourages worker participation in decision-making), we still get feedback about bullies. And the hardest thing in the world is to move against somebody who is delivering the goods but acting 180 degrees from (your values). But if you don't act, you're not walking the talk and you're just an air bag.*

BEING THIRSTY FOR IDEAS

> *We don't claim to be the global fountainhead of management thought, but we may be the world's thirstiest pursuer of big ideas—from whatever their source—and we're not shy about adopting and adapting them. Whether it's QMI from Wal-Mart, or co-location from garage shops, or the "Quick Response" technique from New Zealand, or some blinding insight from some formerly quiet machine operator at a Work-Out session. If it looks like it might make us faster, we try it. And if it works, we spread it across every business in this company—fast.*

FIVE QUESTIONS FOR THE 90S

> *As we look, eagerly, toward '93 and beyond, we ask every person in every business to ask the tough questions leaders must ask themselves every day:*
> *Am I facing reality? Am I seeing the situation the way it really is—or the way I wish, or hope, it were?*

Am I painting flattering self-portraits, or looking honestly in that cold mirror? And when I have grasped the reality, then comes the big, defining question: Am I acting on it fast enough?

Do I see a competitor beating us with lower prices and mutter nervously that "he's nuts" or "he's dumping"—when the real answer is: "He's got lower costs, and I better get my costs down now, or I'm gone"?

Do I see other competitors racing one new product after another into the marketplace and take comfort in deducing they're "spending too much on product development"? *Or do I focus on what they are really doing—increasing the speed of their product development cycle, and beating me to the marketplace?*

Do I wait in hope of some dozing manager suddenly springing into action when he hasn't moved in 10 years? *Do I wish that the autocrat who sits on people all morning and puts barriers between them all afternoon will change his spots? Or is the reality that I lack the courage to make the tough personnel calls that I know I have to make if we're going to win?*

Do I shrug in resignation at slow growth, and wait for new government bureaucrats to replace old government bureaucrats and "fix the economy?" *Or is the reality that slow growth is largely a mind-set that is unknown in start-up businesses and must be unacceptable in big ones?*

Above all, do I recognize the pace of change, which is making obsolete and wrong today what was contemporary and right yesterday? Do I welcome change for the opportunity it always brings—or am I frightened and paralyzed by it?

Translating the need for speed, for reality, into the language and practices that change people's behavior, that encourage them to renew themselves, to walk through that door every day as if it were Monday

morning on a new job—that's what leadership in this company is all about. *No matter how many ideas we try, it all comes back to people—their ideas, their motivation, their passion to win.*

Jack Welch has thought through his business philosophy over the past 12 years. He's had a chance to see what works and what doesn't.

Business leaders without Welch's experience don't have to wait for 12 years to learn from the master. What he's telling you is remarkably straightforward.

For one thing:

Don't convince yourself, before you even begin to work on the problems in your business, that all is lost, that things have grown too complicated, that the time has passed for you to have an impact on the balance sheet.

Welch says it over and over again: Business is just not that complicated.

You, as a business leader, do have to do certain things. But they are not that hard.

First, think about your business vis-à-vis your competitors, and decide what you can do to outsmart your rivals.

Next, don't get in the way of the people who are actually turning out your product. Don't meddle. Let them know at the outset what you expect them to do, then stand aside, and allow them to get on with their work.

It's not complicated.

Oh yes, you can complicate your own life if you don't ask the right questions about your business and your competitors, if you keep interfering with your employees.

If you keep things simple, and manage less, not more, you'll find the payoff will be high.

20

ACT LIKE A SMALL COMPANY!

FROM THE FILES OF *Jack Welch*

"Small companies move faster. They know the penalties for hesitation in the marketplace."

"What we are trying relentlessly to do is get that small-company soul—and small-company speed—inside our big-company body."

It has always been a goal of American corporations to grow—to get big. Bigness is a virtue on the business scene.

Few other companies have grown so large as Jack Welch's General Electric.

Yet, size, with all its virtues, can restrain.

Size can hamper.

Size can inhibit.

This is one of Jack Welch's most important messages.

BIG COMPANIES THAT THINK AND ACT LIKE SMALL COMPANIES WILL DO BETTER

Small companies have clear-cut advantages, and Welch enumerates them:

> *For one,* they communicate better.
> *Without the din and prattle of bureaucracy,* people listen as well as talk; *and since there are fewer of them, they generally know and understand each other.*
> *Second,* small companies move faster. *They know the penalties for hesitation in the marketplace.*
> *Third, in small companies, with fewer layers and less camouflage,* the leaders show up very clearly on the screen. Their performance and its impact are clear to everyone.
> *And, finally,* small companies waste less. *They spend less time in endless reviews and approvals and politics and paper drills. They have fewer people; there-*fore they only do the important things. *Their people are free to direct their energy and attention toward the mar-ketplace rather than fighting bureaucracy.*
> *. . . We find that while we like some of the attrib-utes of big companies—particularly their scale and marketplace reach—it is* small companies that create

excitement, *while big companies, too often, just im-press.*

Most small companies are uncluttered, simple, infor-mal. **They thrive on passion and ridicule bureaucracy. Small companies grow on good ideas—regardless of their source.** *They need everyone, involve everyone, and reward or remove people based on their contribu-tion to winning. Small companies dream big dreams and set the bar high—increments and fractions don't in-terest them.*

We love the way small companies communicate: *with simple, straightforward, passionate argument rather than jargon-filled memos, "putting it in chan-nels," "running it up the flagpole," and, worst of all, the polite deference to the small ideas that too often come from big offices in big companies.*

Everyone in a small company knows the custom-ers—*their likes, dislikes, and needs—because the cus-tomer's thumbs-up or down means the difference be-tween a small company becoming a bigger company tomorrow or no company at all.*

▌ BIGNESS HAS SOME ADVANTAGES

Big allows us, for example, to spend billions on developing the new GE90 jet engine, or the next-generation gas turbine, or Positron Emission Tomogra-phy (PET) diagnostic imaging machines—products that sometimes take years of investment before they begin producing returns.

Size gives us staying power through market cycles in big, promising businesses . . . Size will allow continued heavy investment in new products . . . Size gives us the resources to invest over a half-billion dollars a year on

education: cultivating, at every level in the organiza-
tion, the human capital we must have to win.

Offshore, "big" permits us to form partnerships
with the best of the large companies, and large coun-
tries, and to invest for the long term in nations such as
India, Mexico, and the emerging industrial powers of
South Asia—while still putting billions of dollars into
the research and development of products that will be in
demand in tomorrow's markets.

BUT SIZE NO LONGER IS ENOUGH IN A BRUTALLY COMPETITIVE WORLD MARKETPLACE. BIG COMPANIES HAVE TO ACQUIRE THE SOUL OF A SMALL COMPANY

You keep saying to yourself: But isn't the goal to grow and grow and grow—to become as large a company as possible?

Isn't the goal to get as big as possible so profits will grow?

Sure, the goal is to become more and more profitable.

All Jack Welch is saying is: While you're growing, don't lose sight of the virtues of what small companies offer. While you're growing, don't allow the attributes of bigness to overwhelm you.

Become bigger, but try to emulate a small company as much as possible and you'll be OK.

21
GO FOR THE QUANTUM LEAP!

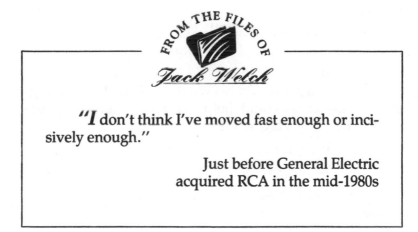

FROM THE FILES OF

Jack Welch

"I don't think I've moved fast enough or incisively enough."

Just before General Electric
acquired RCA in the mid-1980s

Call it the surprise move.

Call it the step that takes you from a so-so company to a spectacular one.

Call it the bold ploy that you took, while others were sitting by, not even contemplating such adventurous gambits.

Surprise, boldness, even shock—those are the elements of the quantum leap.

It's what Jack Welch had in mind as he set out to reshape General Electric.

It's what you should be thinking about as you read how Welch did it through his conquest of RCA.

The purchase of RCA was indeed a surprise move. Throughout much of its history, General Electric had grown from within. It was as though buying an outsider rather than nurturing its own businesses was not playing fair.

It had not been the company's habit to grow by acquisition. Jack Welch discarded that notion.

He wanted to "grow" General Electric's highest-growth businesses, and he would do whatever it took: If buying outside businesses could help, he would buy—and be proud of building a bigger GE.

But not simply for the sake of getting bigger.

Earnings were what mattered to him.

Acquiring businesses that could bolster GE's earnings became a part of the new culture.

By 1985 the Welch revolution was well in stride.

Annual sales were beginning to increase impressively, reaching $28.29 billion that year and making GE the 10th largest company on the Fortune 500 listing, up a notch from the year before.

Most importantly, its earnings had shot up 2 percent in 1985, to $2.336 billion, making GE the fifth most profitable company in America.

The improved earnings were due in no small measure to the $5.6 billion worth of businesses Welch had sold since taking over.

Welch hinted strongly that he would be glad to grab a large company if the fit and the price were right. Then in the mid-80s Jack Welch cast his eyes on RCA, the Radio Corporation of America.

Like General Electric, RCA was one of America's most famous corporate names.

RCA started the National Broadcasting Company in 1926, entered the record industry in 1930, and was the first company to market a television set. RCA had interests in defense electronics, consumer electronics, and satellites as well.

Until the early 1980s, the idea that a General Electric would contemplate grabbing off an NBC, or, for that matter, CBS or ABC, was preposterous.

The three major television networks had always been considered monoliths whose owners would never part with these highly visible, highly profitable properties.

By the fall of 1985 it seemed inevitable that someone would try to grab NBC.

Sometime that year the idea of a merger between General Electric and RCA struck Jack Welch. The NBC television network, which had not been doing well some years earlier, in the mid-1980s was on the upswing.

Performing miracles at NBC in the early 80s, the head of NBC, Grant Tinker, improved the network's ratings with such shows as "Hill Street Blues," "Cheers," "St. Elsewhere," and "Family Ties."

Tinker also supported Brandon Tartikoff's idea for a half-hour comedy with Bill Cosby in 1984. Tartikoff was president of NBC Entertainment.

In 1984 the network's earnings of $248 million accounted for fully 43 percent of RCA's $567 million total. The next year NBC's earnings had climbed to $376 million.

The corporation had turned around, enough to whet the appetite of people like Jack Welch. In the fall he appeared before students at the Harvard Business School.

"If you could change the past," a student asked him, "what would you do differently?"

Quite a question. Why would Welch, having taken General Electric so far in the past four and a half years, want to do anything differently?

The GE chairman thought it over a moment and then, to the surprise of his listeners, confessed, "I don't think I've moved fast enough or incisively enough."

In that single sentence was the hint, the hint of what Welch had been planning to do for months.

His eyes were big.

He wanted to make the big purchase.

To make a quantum leap.

He had always hated it when GE was described as a conglomerate, the implication being one of those corporate giants that bought and sold businesses willy-nilly and was more hodge-podge than focused.

Yet Welch was confident he could buy and sell and remain focused. His goal was not to make GE bigger. It was to add to the company's earnings and value.

The right Big Purchase could, in his view, do just that.

With such thoughts in mind in early November, Jack Welch picked up the phone to Felix Rohatyn, the Wall

Street merger specialist who was a partner with the Lazard Frères investment banking firm.

Rohatyn was friendly with Thornton Bradshaw of RCA. Welch evidently made it clear to Rohatyn that General Electric was interested in acquiring RCA.

Rohatyn played matchmaker and the three men met in Rohatyn's New York City apartment on November 6. They talked for only 45 minutes, making general conversation.

Welch avoided any direct mention that he wanted to buy RCA. But he knew he wanted to buy the company.

After Thanksgiving, "We came back thinking this is the right thing," Welch noted.

General Electric in 1984 had sales of $27.9 billion.

RCA in the same year had $10.1 billion in sales. RCA's electronics business garnered $4.8 billion; its transportation business, $1.4 billion; its entertainment business, $3 billion; its communications business, $400 million; and lesser businesses brought in $300 million.

On December 5 Welch once again met Bradshaw, saying he wanted to buy RCA.

The RCA board met three days later and with only its president and CEO, Robert H. Frederick, dissenting, voted 9 to 1 to pursue the GE talks. Frederick was a former General Electric executive who was in the running for the top RCA job.

Negotiations began the next day.

For RCA staffers, selling David Sarnoff's baby, the home of Nipper, was hard to swallow.

Would the RCA brand name be subsumed under the General Electric logo?

A highly defensive Jack Welch brooked no criticism of the deal.

"You now have an enterprise that is totally unique—in the world."

December 12, 1985.

Jack Welch called a press conference at the General Electric building in Manhattan and journalists showed up in droves.

It was Jack Welch's boldest move.

And General Electric's.

Crotonville's Jim Baughman called it the biggest counterculture step Jack Welch's GE had ever taken.

GE and RCA had agreed that GE would purchase the communications giant for $6.28 billion, or $66.50 a share.

It was the largest non-oil merger ever.

General Electric ranked ninth of America's largest industrial firms. RCA was second among the nation's service firms.

Together they formed a new corporate power with sales of $40 billion, placing it seventh on the Fortune 500, a step behind IBM but ahead of Du Pont.

"This is going to be one dynamite company," boasted Welch.

With some Wall Street analysts putting the value of RCA's businesses at $90 a share, GE appeared to be getting a great bargain.

Everyone from the business experts to the comedians had an opinion of the merger.

Johnny Carson, host of NBC's "Tonight Show," joked, "It's a break for me. The last person who hosted a GE show did very well," referring to Ronald Reagan's hosting of the GE Theater in the 50s.

Jokes aside, Jack Welch was buoyant about the new company's prospects.

He was confident the merger would buttress General Electric's drive into the service and technology fields—and would diminish its dependence on manufacturing businesses.

After the merger GE expected to obtain 80 percent of its earnings from service and technology businesses. That helped to fulfill one of Welch's original goals from the early 80s.

The fit seemed ideal. GE and RCA seemed natural partners in defense contracting: General Electric had been building aircraft engines and guidance systems for ICBMs; RCA had made electronic equipment for the Navy's missile-launching cruisers.

That synergy would turn the new merged firm into a stronger competitor for "Star Wars" contracts. That RCA's two largest businesses (broadcasting and defense) were largely free from foreign competition appealed enormously to Welch. NBC had other dividends: It required little investment and generated much cash.

MORE THAN ANYTHING ELSE, THE MERGER MADE GENERAL ELECTRIC A GLOBAL COMPANY.

"We will have the technological capabilities, financial resources and global scope," declared Welch, "to be able to compete successfully with anyone, anywhere, in every market we serve . . ."

Other synergies were expected from the two companies' consumer electronics businesses. Both sold television sets and radios: RCA, with a $4.8 billion business, was far larger than GE's at $1 billion.

Reaction at NBC was mixed.

Although GE had the reputation of an outsider within the broadcasting industry, it had owned eight radio stations, three television stations and a cable television system, but by 1983 had sold most of those properties.

NBC News executives and correspondents worried that General Electric might meddle with the way the news was presented, that their cherished independence would be compromised. Determined to ease their discomfort, Welch promised that "the traditional independence of NBC News' operation will be maintained."

Entertainment accounted for 30 percent of RCA's sales of $10.1 billion and 40 percent of its net profit of $246.4 million in 1984.

NBC was on the verge of winning the prime-time ratings race for the first time.

The hits just kept coming: "Golden Girls," "Alf," "Matlock," "L.A. Law," "Amen." The blockbuster was "The Cosby Show," which at times enjoyed a 50 share—one out of every two TV sets in use was tuned in to "Cosby."

Winning the season was Grant Tinker's grand moment.

Welch thought Tinker and his crowd the greatest. "They're our type of people. They know how to be number one, and we know how to give people who know how to be number one money."

At first blush Tinker appeared pleased with the new owners. "They are good managers at General Electric, and good managers usually subscribe to the theory that if it ain't broke, don't fix it, and NBC ain't broke."

Despite all the nice words, a fear lingered that this huge industrial firm called General Electric would frighten its competitors off from advertising on the network.

Concern also persisted that, as a major defense contractor, GE would want to censor NBC's coverage of defense news.

The thrust of all this worry was that General Electric might use its newly acquired position as a media giant to influence all kinds of decisions, some major, some minor, that affected the company.

JACK WELCH HAD HIS QUANTUM LEAP.

Now the task before him was to "impose" the GE culture on his new acquisition.

It would not be easy.

22

NO MATTER HOW GREAT THE RESISTANCE, GET THOSE COSTS DOWN!

FROM THE FILES OF

Jack Welch

*"I*f you do not change, I'll guarantee you, there's somebody else out there who will want to do it."

Nowhere were Jack Welch's business ideas tested more than at the NBC television network.

GE had its own business culture. NBC had its own. Now the two would confront one another.

Which one would triumph?

The battle would reveal not only whether Welch could push his business ideas throughout all of General Electric, but it also would demonstrate whether it was possible for a large corporation to impose its culture on a recalcitrant, cantankerous, independent-minded business division.

While the battle occurred, the whole world seemed to be watching. That added to the drama, the controversy, and the stakes.

At issue, as in most great business disputes, was the question of money. Or more precisely, how much NBC should be allowed to spend.

For years the three great television networks in America had functioned without having to worry about costs. The networks were glamorous, they were profitable, and they were seemingly immutable to any bottom-line pressures.

They commanded huge audiences and had a near monopoly on television viewing around the nation.

If you worked for NBC, or CBS, or ABC, you automatically deserved a big salary and lots of perks.

Then along came Jack Welch in the mid-80s. All he wanted from NBC was what he wanted from his aircraft engines business or his lighting business:

- **To be profitable.**

- **To be careful with expenditures—in short, to be productive.**

- **To fit into the General Electric culture.**

In the case of NBC, Welch looked at its profits and asked a simple question: How was it that the network that had the highest ratings also had the lowest profits?

Welch could not understand how NBC could justify all those high costs.

To the people at NBC, the answer was self-evident. Television was glamorous. Making light bulbs was not.

Besides, NBC was on a roll. In September 1986 NBC won 34 Emmy awards, the most NBC had ever won. More importantly, the network was enjoying record-breaking profits that were 54 percent ahead of 1984.

Nonetheless, NBC President Robert Wright, a Welch appointee brought in to spread the GE culture through the network, spent his first days in the job calming nerves.

"General Electric," he asserted lightly, "simply wants me to take the best and make it better."

And cheaper.

NBC had become, in the wake of Bob Wright's appointment, a seething cauldron of anxieties and fears.

Wright knew this and seemed to understand the rage. Nonetheless, he was not their favorite person.

Wright may have denied at the outset that he was going to shake NBC up, but it was inevitable and could not be kept a secret.

The chemistry between Wright and NBC did not work well. Clashes were inevitable. One insider noted:

> *One of the difficulties in the coming together of GE and NBC was that the GE guys, probably flowing from Welch's style, had a view of management by confrontation. I should say management by provocation ... The GE people were up to this free for all. The NBC people*

were not ... Welch would ... bring these guys up to Fairfield to discuss budgets—confront them, ask them tough questions. They were unhinged by that.

The clashes began, not surprisingly, when Bob Wright asked each division to plan budget reductions of 5 percent.

The primary resistance came from NBC executives, including the president of NBC News, Lawrence K. Grossman.

NBC News had enjoyed a string of fat years. The budget, which had been "only" $207.3 million in 1983, had mushroomed to $282.5 million in 1984 and was around that level when GE took over.

Advertising on NBC's news programs was supposed to cover the news budget but never equaled the news division's expenses, reaching no more than $250 million a year in the mid-80s, (half of that from the "NBC Nightly News").

Grossman made it clear to Wright that he could not afford to cut $15 million.

Wright was not impressed. Nor were others at GE.

In Wright's and Welch's eyes, NBC News was the bad guy in the cost department.

While it produced only 10 percent of the network's revenues, its $277 million budget for 1986 was 16 percent of the network's costs.

In that year NBC News lost $80 million.

Estimates were that the losses would rise to between $120 and $130 million later in the 80s. In 1988, the year Michael Gartner was hired to replace Grossman as NBC News president, the news operation lost $126 million.

What was going on at the network stymied Jack Welch.

He knew that Ted Turner at CNN was airing 24 hours of news a day for only $100 million, and Turner was making a profit of $50 to $60 million.

In the mid-1980s, his own NBC had been airing only three hours of news a day, spending about $275 million and losing almost $100 million. How could that be?

NBC News executives admitted to Wright and Welch that they had no real budget plan. These executives had never been expected to present one to the big brass. That had been handled by others.

The executives did not like the losses. They made clear that they planned to deal with them—sometime in the far-off future. It was no wonder Larry Grossman got on Jack Welch's nerves.

Grossman tried to suggest to Welch that NBC News, because it was a public trust, should not have to face the same bottom-line pressures of other GE business units.

Welch exploded.

As the chief executive officer of General Electric, he too had a public trust, Welch asserted, and it was a million times more important than the one at NBC News. His public trust had to do with refrigerators that could explode, airplanes that could crash. His customers put their lives in Jack Welch's hands, pretty high stakes. Larry Grossman ought to consider Welch's situation when he talked of the network being a public trust.

Welch went apoplectic when Grossman, after being asked to trim the budget by 5 percent, weighed in with a request for a 4 percent hike above the 1986 budget.

Grossman got Welch's message.

At a fateful meeting with Welch on November 16, 1986, Grossman agreed to maintain his 1987 budget at the same level as 1986, which was in fact a drop of about 5 percent with inflation factored in.

Wright would win the battle.

He was the boss.

He had the full backing of Jack Welch.

But would he win the war?

Would he figure out how to win over the hearts of those who stayed behind?

Would the profits that he would coax out of the business be worth the heartache and frustration that he would cause throughout the rank and file?

These were questions he dared not ask himself at the time of the worst cost-cutting.

Bob Wright won the early skirmishes.

Whatever controversies arose in those first few years of his tenure, however much blood was spilled, if the bottom line was all that counted to Wright and to Jack Welch, then the two men should have been infinitely happy.

In 1991 Wright crowed:

> *There's probably never been anything like it. There's no company in broadcasting that's ever enjoyed as much success as we enjoyed in the last five years.*

In 1985 NBC had a profit of $333 million. In 1986, the year Wright took over, profits reached $350 million. NBC's revenues were over the $3 billion mark for the first time.

NBC was first place in the ratings. The "Today" show was ranked first and so was "NBC Nightly News with Tom Brokaw."

Wright and Welch had much to celebrate.

The financial picture improved even more in the late 80s.

NBC's profits reached $410 million in 1987, $500 million in 1988, $750 million in 1989, and $500 million in 1990.

The cost-cutting had worked.

Other NBC businesses, including cable and a home video venture with Columbia Pictures, brought in cash.

Most importantly, the seven NBC-owned television stations were profitable. In 1987 they earned $200 million, half of NBC's total. From 1979 to 1987 their compound annual profit growth came to 20 percent, making them one of General Electric's best businesses.

Welch, however, could not tolerate NBC's cavalier approach to excising fat and waste.

In late March 1987 at a closed session in Florida, he blasted NBC executives for being rooted in the past. If they did not change, he warned, "I'll guarantee you, there's somebody out there who will want to do it."

Welch sought to put NBC into a GE perspective.

He was proud of what the network had accomplished, but NBC was only one player among 13 very big players.

He warned the 100 NBC executives assembled that managers in other GE-owned businesses who had resisted joining the culture had been "sent home."

They could not face the change in the world, "and nowhere do I feel it as deeply as in this room."

Welch wanted NBC to adopt a strict business discipline.

Ironically, of the three networks, only NBC was expected to show a profit for that year.

No one in the audience appreciated Welch's next comment.

While NBC had some good people, it also had some "turkeys."

General Electric wanted to provide those good people with the chance "to chase and search for those who are hiding under the umbrella" and get rid of them.

Meanwhile, the institution that was once known as the Radio Corporation of America was disappearing.

After the merger, GE sold most of what had been left of RCA. What remained were the NBC television network, five NBC-owned television stations, and the Defense Electronics Division.

Even the RCA name was removed from 30 Rockefeller Plaza at Rockefeller Center in New York. It became the General Electric building.

By the summer of 1987, GE had cut the number of RCA employees from 87,577 to 35,900 through dismissals or the sale of assets.

One of the hardest blows for RCA fans to absorb was the loss of the radio network.

In one of life's ironies, the National Broadcasting Company had been founded in 1926 by the Radio Corporation of America, Westinghouse, and General Electric.

NBC became the largest of the early radio networks. For many years it carried "Amos 'n' Andy," the most widely listened to program in America, as well as "Fibber McGee and Molly." Its stars included Jack Benny and George Burns and Gracie Allen.

The network distributed programming to more than 700 stations around the country. In time, however, it was undermined by the advent of television.

In the summer of 1987, the radio network was sold to Westwood One for $50 million. Not included in the sale were the eight NBC-owned radio stations.

The sale came as a shock to NBC employees because the radio station had been an RCA treasure.

Nearly as distressing, under the sale's terms, Westwood could continue to use the network's name.

In other words Welch had sold the name NBC News to another firm. The transaction also agitated NBC television staff who now believed General Electric might be tempted to sell its other "treasure"—the television network.

As NBC moved into the 90s, the television business was getting tougher and tougher. Profits began to skid as advertisers turned away from the networks and toward other ways of reaching consumers, including cable television and direct mail. Cable and other media continued to compete for viewers.

Ironically, throughout 1990 NBC was the number one-rated network.

Yet by that summer the financial picture was less bright. NBC's revenues had fallen by 4.6 percent to $3.2 billion. Profits had fallen also by 21 percent to $477 million.

In 1991 NBC's profits were some $300 million, down from the previous few years.

The Persian Gulf war had cost NBC $60 million in extra news costs and lost advertising revenue.

Ratings had fallen too.

Newspapers speculated that NBC was in play, and Wright acknowledged he had listened to proposals about the network's future from investment banking firms.

By the spring former NBC executives rushed into print with complaints that GE had damaged the place irreparably.

One former NBC executive was quoted as saying: "All the people who care are gone. People either still there, or who just left, in Burbank or New York, say it's not the same company."

NBC had logged its sixth straight triumph, finishing the 1990–1991 television season in first place in the closest rating race in almost three decades.

But for the first time, NBC was no longer the top choice of advertisers with products for men and women aged 18 to 49. ABC was.

Although NBC seemed to occupy a disproportionate amount of Welch's time in 1991, he claimed to have spent no more time on the network than he did on appliances or medical technologies. Was it clearly the most cantankerous of his 13 businesses?

He would only admit that NBC was "the most exciting, the most intriguing, the fattest, in terms of its overhead structure, the most set in its ways, unwilling to change."

In October 1991 Bob Wright was still pushing for change at NBC.

> *If anything, we moved too slowly, all three of us. We at NBC got accused of moving too fast. I'll criticize myself that we've moved too slowly. That the marketplace has changed so dramatically and we aren't well enough positioned to deal with it as we should. We are very much in danger of being eradicated, and I still after five years here have not been able to convince people enough that that's a fact. We are suffering essentially the same fate as the big three automotives. We can be a big participant (in broadcasting), but we will be an unprofitable big participant. We can either try to structure ourselves as a business going forward, which we will be a much more modest business than we have been; or we can remain enormously visible, probably at a very unacceptable level of profitability.*

The early 1990s were rough years for NBC. After several years as America's number one-rated network, NBC ended 1992 in third place. The network was steeped in controversy as well. In February 1993 NBC was forced to apologize on the air to General Motors Corp. for rigging a demonstration crash of GM's pickup trucks on the "Dateline" NBC program. Three weeks later, NBC News President Michael Gartner resigned.

Also in 1993, the popular late-night talk-show host David Letterman left NBC to go to CBS.

Financially, NBC News seemed to be doing better. After losing money in the 1980s, its projected earnings for 1993 were $20 million. The overall network projected earnings of $275 million, 12 percent ahead of its 1992 profits.

Yet speculation persisted that Jack Welch was interested in selling the network. Periodically, newspaper stories suggested a deal was in the offing. Nothing happened. For the time being, Welch seemed content with NBC.

He had tamed the wild beast, and it gave him some satisfaction that the network was making a decent, if not an outstanding, profit.

The powerful lesson for you, the business leader, in all of this is:

As you pursue the goal of cutting costs, you will likely meet opposition.

Arguments will be made by those who want to stave off the cost-cutting that seem logical, compelling, persuasive.

Welch saw through all the arguments thrown at him by the NBC crowd. They were arguments based on the way things were done in the past.

That was one strong reason Welch didn't like the past, why he thought the past held few lessons for him.

When thinking about cutting costs—or any business step that is unpleasant, painful, and seems to go against the grain of logic—keep your eye on the company s future.

The past is no guide. It's what got you into this situation in the first place.

23

GET FASTER!

FROM THE FILES OF
Jack Welch

*"S*peed is everything. It is the indispensable ingredient in competitiveness."

To survive in today's competitive world, according to Jack Welch, big companies like General Electric must acquire the habits and style of small companies.

What Jack Welch admires most about the behavior of small companies is their speed.

> **Speed is everything.** *It is the indispensable ingredient in competitiveness. Speed keeps businesses—and people—young. It's addictive, and it's a profoundly American taste we need to cultivate.*

Welch is in love with the idea of speed. Just listen to him wax poetic on the subject:

> *There is something about speed that transcends its obvious business benefits of greater cash flows, greater profitability, higher share due to greater customer responsiveness and more capacity from cycle time reductions.*
>
> *Speed exhilarates and energizes ... This is particularly true in business, where speed tends to propel ideas and drive processes right through functional barriers, sweeping bureaucrats and their impediments aside in the rush to get to the marketplace.*

▌ BEFORE IT'S TOO LATE, ACT TO SPEED UP THE WAY YOUR BUSINESS WORKS

> *That's what the best companies do best, and our challenge at GE for '93 and beyond is clear—to ignite this big company with* passion, hunger, appetite for change, customer focus, and, above all, the speed to see reality more clearly and to act on it faster.

Companies and countries, argues Welch, appear to follow predictable life cycles. At their start, new businesses are gripped by an urgency to rush to the marketplace. In an environment like that, bureaucracy cannot get a foothold in the same way that ice cannot form in a fast-moving stream.

> *But as institutions prosper and get more comfortable, the priority begins to shift gradually from speed to control; from leading to managing; from winning to conserving what has been won; from serving the customer to serving the bureaucracy.*
>
> *We begin to erect layers of management to smooth decision making and control and that growth, and all it does, is slow us down. We put barriers between the functions of our businesses, which create turf and fiefdom.*

Before a company can figure out how to act more speedily, it must clear away the barriers that slow it down.

In Short, Get Rid of the Bureaucracy!

> *While we have made real progress in the assault on bureaucracy, we can never let up. Bureaucracy and bureaucrats have to be ridiculed and removed . . . (Bureaucracy) distracts and disengages good minds from productive activity. It favors those who control over those who contribute. It throttles productivity growth.*
>
> *If you're not fast, you can't win. You must get products to market faster and response from customers quicker. You've got to make decisions fast. If you're not boundaryless, and you've got a bunch of (management) layers, that's like going out in the cold with six sweaters on. Your body doesn't know what the temperature is.*

SPEED IS A VACCINE AGAINST BUREAUCRACY

Speed, which brings with it an urgency, an exhilaration and a focus on what really matters, is a vaccine against bureaucracy and lethargy. It is the simple ingredient that drives small companies, and it is the lack of speed that gets big companies in trouble.

AN EXAMPLE OF SPEED AT GE: QUICK RESPONSE

Quick Response. This is a cycle-time reduction technique we adapted from our Canadian affiliate, which found it in an appliance company in New Zealand, which got it from who knows where. Quick Response erases most of the barriers between the functions of our businesses—manufacturing, finance, etc.—and the customers and has taken GE Appliances from an 18-week order-to-deliver cycle to a 3½-week cycle at the present—on the way to three days. Quick Response has reduced average inventory in GE Appliances 50 percent, or almost $400 million, and will allow it to break through the 10-turn barrier in 1993—almost double the rate of 1989.

But, how do you get that speed in a $60 billion company with 230,000 employees competing all over the earth? Before you begin to accelerate an organization, you have to take the brakes off. The brakes in our case are the boundaries, the barriers, the fiefdoms, the remnants of a bureaucracy that slow us down.

AN EXAMPLE OF SPEED AT GE:

Quick market intelligence is a boundary-busting technique aimed at measuring the pulse of the marketplace

*and redirecting us to meet customer needs. It is fast be-
coming the heart and soul of how GE businesses work,
leading to speed and customer satisfaction.*

▌ QUICK MARKET INTELLIGENCE

*It is a process that gives every salesperson direct ac-
cess, every Friday, to the key managers and the CEO of
the business, to lay out customer problems and needs.
The product of the meeting is not deep or strategic in nature, but action—a response to the customer right
away. The QMI routine turns the face of everyone in the
organization toward the marketplace and, by doing so,
makes the bureaucracy stand out for what it really is:
silly, irrelevant, and even malevolent in its interference
in the process of serving customers.*

In June 1993 Welch extolled the virtues of QMI:

*"This is going to change this company. Wal-Mart
started with one store and translated it to 2,000 stores.
That's a helluva lot easier than what we're doing. We're
taking a 115-year-old bureaucracy and trying to get it
close to the customer. (Wal-Mart copied one store.) So
our job is tough. We still get: "Do I have to be there?"
Can you imagine anyone saying that? Do I have to do
that? . . . It's the craziest conversation in the world. But
we still have it. We've got to root that out. No one in
this room should not be deeply involved in QMI.*

*If you're not, you're out of here. Within two years
we will have eliminated half of the meetings we have in
this company. This (QMI) will be the meeting that runs
the whole company. It will be the heart and soul of the
company, the driver behind growth.*

It's . . . finding a better way every day . . . it involves every function, all people, all layers, all aimed at meeting customer needs.

Too many people in big companies come through the gate each morning to serve the internal bureaucracy. Customers—if they are thought of at all—are some vague abstraction.

QMI CHANGES ALL THAT.

Why is speed so important, Welch asked in June 1993?

Because you have a competitive world. You've got to get the product at the right time, to the right person, at the right place, fast. You've got to be able to do that. You've got to be able to respond.

You may be skeptical about Jack Welch's love affair with the notion of speed.

Speed, you say to yourself, can get you into trouble.

It can lower quality.

It can disrupt your business's crucial command-and-control systems.

It can cause serious organizational errors to occur in getting the product from the factory to the consumer.

Jack Welch knows all that—and he has answers for you.

He's not talking about developing speed at the price of lowering quality, disrupting command-and-control systems, or organizational slowdowns.

Welch is talking about keeping up all these standards—and at the same time figuring out how to get faster.

He's saying big businesses can become slothful. Some of that sloth may be inherent because of the company's large size. But some of it may not be.

Welch's advice to you is this: Don't simply assume all sloth is inherent.

You can make things move more speedily.

All you have to do is search for those areas in the company where processes serve no purpose other than slowing things down.

If you look hard enough, you will find them.

24

REMOVE THE BOUNDARIES!

25

SEARCH FOR THE SYNERGIES BETWEEN YOUR BUSINESSES—STRIVE FOR INTEGRATED DIVERSITY

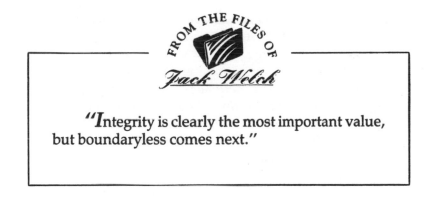

*"I*ntegrity is clearly the most important value, but boundaryless comes next."

It took Jack Welch time to develop the idea.

When he did, the word he chose to describe what he meant was—and he would be the first to admit it—awkward and clumsy. Yet it seemed to sum up what he wanted to convey neatly and effectively.

After all his talk of paring down GE, after he spelled out the need for getting rid of bureaucratic layers, it occurred to Jack Welch that what he really wanted to do was to make General Electric

BOUNDARYLESS.

Yes, it was an awkward, clumsy word. But, to Welch, it sounded right. In a speech he made in March 1990, he articulates what is behind the notion:

> *The pace of change will be felt in several areas. Globalization is now no longer an objective but an imperative, as markets open and geographic barriers become increasingly blurred and even irrelevant . . .*
>
> *Simply doing more of what worked in the 80s—the restructuring, the delayering, the mechanical, top-down measures that we took—will be too incremental. More than that, it will be too slow.* **The winners of the 90s will be those who can develop a culture that allows them to move faster, communicate more clearly, and involve everyone in a focused effort to serve ever more demanding customers.**
>
> *To move toward that winning culture we've got to create what we call a* **boundaryless** *company. We no longer have the time to climb over barriers between functions like engineering and marketing, or between people—hourly, salaried, management, and the like. Geographic barriers must evaporate.* **Our people must be as comfortable in Delhi and Seoul as they are in Louisville or Schenectady . . .**

Welch, in a speech he gave on April 24, 1990, asked how a company gets faster, what stands between a company and the speed it needs.

> *In designing a high-performance airplane, engineers work incessantly at eliminating or flattening any protruding surfaces that produce a drag. The result is a clean design that moves quickly and smoothly through the air. In a company the drag comes from* **boundaries**— *the walls that grow between functions such as finance and marketing and manufacturing;* **boundaries between** *suppliers and the company; between the company and customers. Each of these* **boundaries** *is a speed bump that slows the enterprise. Each piece of turf within these boundary walls is defended by the watchdogs of bureaucracy.*

How do you get rid of these boundaries?

The vertical ones—layer after layer of management, Jack Welch said, were relatively easy targets, and GE had reduced or compressed them substantially in the 80s.

> *The horizontal ones, primarily between functions, are much more difficult. The barriers between them grow, basically, because of insecurity.*

What is **the boundaryless company?**

It is, says Jack Welch, one in which

> *We knock down the walls that separate us from each other on the inside and from our key constituents on the outside.*

The Boundaryless Company

- Removes barriers between functions.

- Removes barriers between levels.

- Removes barriers between locations.

- Reaches out to important suppliers and makes them part of a single process in which "they and we join hands and intellects in a common purpose—satisfying customers."

Boundarylessness, Jack Welch argues, is the only way to achieve General Electric's productivity goals.

Boundarylessness was far more than merely getting rid of bureaucratic waste.

> *Ultimately, we're talking about redefining the relationship between boss and subordinate.*
> *Instead of hierarchy, there will be* **cross-functional teams.**
> *Instead of managers, there will be* **business leaders.**
> *Instead of workers being told what to do, workers will be* **empowered** *and given responsibility.*
> *My view of the 1990s is based on the* **liberation of the workplace.** *If you want to get the benefit of everything employees have, you've got to free them—make everybody a participant. Everybody has to know everything, so they can make the right decisions by themselves.*

By the time he penned his annual report of 1992, Welch was effusive about "boundarylessness." Here is what he said:

This behavior definer (boundarylessness) led us to a process called Work-Out that we've been using for four years now to capture good ideas and run with them— whether their originator is a crane operator on the line or some company on the other side of the Earth. Work-Out has been the vehicle that has allowed us to act on a series of innovative ways of removing barriers—always with an eye to becoming faster—becoming better.

CO-LOCATION

Co-location is the ultimate boundaryless behavior and is as unsophisticated as can be: We tear all the walls down and put teams from all functions together in one room to bring new products to life. One room, one coffeepot, one team, one shared mission.

The standard lament of manufacturing—"What idiot designed this thing?"—is no longer heard because the product is now designed with manufacturing, with marketing, with suppliers, and often with the customers themselves.

GE Medical Systems is using this boundaryless technique to design and manufacture its new ultrasound products. The Profile appliance line was developed this way, as was the GE90 jet engine. Before long it will be the way GE develops everything it makes, and every service it sells.

He said in the summer of 1992:

"Boundarylessness, there's that ugly, long word again. You've got to be able to be as comfortable with a

Jakarta worker, with Bandung's aircraft engine factory as you are seeing Suharto two hours later. We don't have any right because we have a title or position. We are obligated to be part of a constituency that is all pulling together to win. There is no boundary, there is no hierarchy; it's a place for ideas. Ideas are what counts. It's what you bring to the party that counts.

Then, in a speech he gave to the New England Council in November 1992:

"Boundarylessness" ... *means engaging every mind on every problem, leaving no one out, weighing no one's ideas heavier because of the color of their collar or their skin, their gender, their nationality, or whatever.*

We find again and again that every barrier that divides us, between engineering and manufacturing, between us and suppliers or us and customers, between the preconceived view we have of Jakarta or Shanghai and the view we know of Boston or Des Moines, between genders, between races, every barrier—serious or silly—is a speed bump that slows us down and deprives us of the quickness we must have to capture the opportunity that is out there in abundance.

Jack Welch spoke to the General Electric Annual Meeting of Share Owners in Fort Wayne, Indiana, on April 18, 1993, describing in depth what he means by

THE BOUNDARYLESS COMPANY.

GE is doing well and is positioned to do even better in the future, not because of some sophisticated strategy or some technology breakthrough or even, as some have

said, because of the depth and strength of its manage-
ment. On the contrary, one of the reasons we are doing
so well is not because we are managing better but be-
cause we are managing less—and that is better.

HORIZONTAL BOUNDARIES

One kind are the horizontal boundaries, the bounda-
ries between suppliers and ourselves, between cus-
tomers and ourselves, and between ourselves—where,
typically, marketing specifies a product and hands it to
engineering, which designs it and hands it to manufac-
turing to produce—in a long, slow, sequential chain.
Suppliers and customers outside our boundaries
were traditionally left out of this process. Now we're
trying to do things with everybody involved—every-
body contributing ideas simultaneously, from suppliers
to customers, from beginning to end.

VERTICAL BOUNDARIES

Then there are the vertical boundaries, the hierarchi-
cal organizational layers that proliferate in big institu-
tions. Layers insulate. They slow things down. They
garble communications.

By the summer of 1993, boundaryless had become one
of the core values at General Electric:

If you're turf-oriented, self-centered, don't share
with people and are not searching for ideas, you don't
belong here. . . . Being boundaryless allows us to jab one

another and have fun. We rag each other when some-
body starts to protect turf. An organization has to be
informal, relaxed and trusting.

One of the more important examples of boundarylessness at GE is the way General Electric's businesses behave
toward one another, always seeking synergies, always trying to prove the sum is greater than the parts. Welch calls
this notion "integrated diversity."

He originally promoted the idea to refute the conten-
tion that GE was just another conglomerate.

> *We're not even close to being a conglomerate. A con-*
> *glomerate is a group of businesses with no central*
> *theme. GE has a common set of values. We have Cro-*
> *tonville, where we teach leadership. We have a research*
> *lab that feeds all of our businesses. We have all the re-*
> *sources of a centralized company. Yet we've been able to*
> *go in and out of businesses for more than a century and*
> *stay ahead of changing times.*

All kinds of synergies exist at GE, Welch says. General
Electric, from the time it diversified beyond its core of electrical manufacturing businesses, always made a great effort to move human, financial, and technical resources
around the company.

In the past GE would transfer a manager from aircraft
engines to lighting if an opening arose. Under Welch that
happened as well, but he would also take teams from different businesses and move them back and forth to help
one another out of problems.

During the late 80s and early 90s, Welch sought to ex-
tract as much integrated diversity from GE as possible.

One business that was caught by the "diversity" bug was GE Capital. It oversaw the financing of all sorts of equipment built by other GE businesses, including commercial aircraft engines, locomotives, and power generation.

Another great source of synergy at GE was the Research and Development Center in Schenectady.

Imaging technology developed for medical systems turned into a highly efficient piece of equipment for inspecting jet engines in the aircraft engines business. Highly sophisticated machining and coating techniques designed for the aircraft engines business wound up in power generation as well. And so on.

You're probably getting the idea by now.

Welch's business philosophy aims in part at dismantling all the obstacles inside one's own business that hamper the successful marketing of your products.

For you, the business leader, one of Welch's more important messages is to look closely at your company and ask yourself: What parts of the business are slowing us down?

To answer that question, you will have to take a fresh look at all the processes in your business. Then ask: Are these processes helping to move the product along to the marketplace speedily?

Or are these processes just bottling things up?

Ask these questions and you will be on the right track to business success.

Answer these questions in the right way, and you will find quick improvements in your business.

26

EMPOWER YOUR WORKERS!

FROM THE FILES OF

Jack Welch

*"T*he way to harness the power of these people is to protect them, not to sit on them, but to turn them loose, let them go—get the management layers off their backs, the bureaucratic shackles off their feet and the function barriers out of their way."

"The way to get faster, more productive, and more competitive is to unleash the energy and intelligence and raw, ornery, self-confidence of the American worker, who is still by far the most productive and innovative in the world."

The first phase of Jack Welch's revolution at General Electric had occurred during the early 1980s.

It had brought massive change. Among those changes:

- 350 businesses had been transformed into 13.

- The core electrical manufacturing businesses were no longer the focus of the company.

- High-tech and service segments were the focus.

- Plants had been shut.

- Buildings had been leveled.

- Existing factories had been made state of the art.

- New plants had been built.

- Layers of management had been cast aside.

- The company had fewer employees (down 25 percent to 300,000) but larger revenues and earnings.

Jack Welch called these years "**The Hardware Phase**."

While it aided General Electric's bottom line, the hardware phase had left the company's employees disconcerted.

Many of their reference points had been cut from under them.

They worked in new plants, had new bosses, new jobs. Often the jobs they had hoped to attain through promotion no longer existed.

In the meantime, new people came along and competed for the fewer promotions that remained. All these changes proved disorienting to the survivors of the hardware phase.

By the late 1980s, Jack Welch sensed he needed to push the revolution in a different direction. A serious issue confronted him.

Though much smaller, GE's workforce would be expected to achieve even greater productivity. Yet the company was still trembling from the earthquake of downsizing.

Now that GE employees no longer had the promise of a job for life, how could Jack Welch guarantee that the surviving workforce would be motivated to work as hard as before?

Because of downsizing, it would be hard to persuade employees their work burden had been reduced. Yet some way had to be found that would make them feel less like overworked cogs in a machine and more like "owners" of the business.

By the fall of 1988, Jack Welch was ready to start the second phase of his revolution.

The best path seemed to be **delegating authority to the employees**. That would be an important first step.

Jack Welch outlined his ideas on empowerment in a speech he gave November 11, 1992, to the New England Council in Boston, Massachusetts.

People say that now that the Soviet Union is out of business we have no more truly dangerous enemies. They're wrong. The Soviets couldn't beat us, but economically, the bureaucracy and bureaucrats still can.

The way to get faster, more productive, and more competitive is to unleash the energy and intelligence and raw, ornery, self-confidence of the American worker, who is still by far the most productive and innovative in the world.

The way to harness the power of these people is to protect them, not to sit on them, but to turn them loose, let them go—get the management layers off their backs, the bureaucratic shackles off their feet and the function barriers out of their way.

Whereas in the past, the managers had been responsible for improving productivity, now this would become the task of the men and women on the factory floor.

Welch called it

EMPOWERMENT.

Before at GE, we generally used to tell people what to do. And they did exactly what they were told to do, and not one other thing. Now we are constantly amazed by how much people will do when they are not told what to do by management.

This was a new concept.

"For 25 years," a middle-aged hourly worker in the major appliances business declared, "you've paid for my hands when you could have had my brain—for nothing."

It would not be easy for GE to abandon its tight supervision and control over employees.

Autocratic managers would find it bizarre to suddenly let workers on the floor make decisions, contribute ideas, organize their workdays. As GE managers liked to say, they had been used to workers who parked their brains at the factory gate each morning.

Rather than joining hands in a common effort to improve the business, management and labor had always looked at each other through a prism of venom.

"We spent 90 percent of our time on the floor figuring out how to screw the management," an employee told Jack Welch in the spring of 1991. "That was all right, because you guys spent 95 percent of your time figuring out how to screw us."

Even at its most benign, the relationships between managers and employees lacked camaraderie. Managers dictated, employees obeyed.

> *"General Electric," said Wally Croote, an area machinist in the power generation business in Schenectady, "didn't want any reaction from the employees. I used to come to work and stand in front of a podium and wait for the foreman to tell me where to work . . . I would never catch myself going to the manager if I had a complaint. I went to the union. It didn't matter if Moses were the foreman."*

Could Jack Welch assuage that anger?

Could he take the Wally Crootes of General Electric and use their brain power?

Would making the workday pleasant for the floor worker make him or her more productive?

Welch came to believe that relying on the gray matter of the labor force to solve the day-to-day problems on the factory floors might be the way to fire up employees emerging from the mayhem and anguish of restructuring.

By making them feel that they had a stake in the company's future, Welch might inject a spirit of common purpose that would impress outsiders.

He remained troubled by Wall Street's assessment of his business strategies as ineffectual in creating focus and coherence at GE. Blaming himself, Welch sensed that more had to be done than write articulate letters to share owners in the annual report.

Welch had a tinge of regret that he had waited seven years to empower his workforce.

The one consolation was that starting earlier would have been impractical.

GE was in too much ferment, too many stomachs were churning each morning as workers wondered whether their jobs were on the line.

Thousands of employees were leaving the place, thousands more joining the GE ranks.

Amid such uncertainty and sweeping change, employees would not have been receptive to a corporate plan to make them more productive and give them cheer.

Welch sensed this:

> *Empowering and liberating and exhilarating a bloated bureaucracy in the beginning would have been impossible. It would have produced a mixed message because we were shocking them. I'm not sure you could have sold that and been credible.*

So he waited until 1988.

Then he unleashed the next phase of his revolution.

He called it Work-Out.

Work-Out, as we shall see in a while, is all about propping up your employees, making them feel good, making them feel as if they are contributing directly to the overall goals of the company.

As hard as it may be for you, as a business leader, to dismiss an employee, it may be equally difficult for you to turn over decision making to the employees who remain behind.

But that is exactly what Jack Welch is advocating. Not out of an altruistic impulse to be nice to one's employees. Not out of some sense that you, as the business leader, aren't as smart as the employees on the factory floor.

Welch is saying something else: Treat your employees as an integral part of the business, and you will find that they, in turn, will become more productive.

You will find that the business will benefit.

As alien as it seems to turn over "management" prerogatives to your employees, try it.

Adopt the Jack Welch philosophy of empowering your employees. Give it a chance.

You should find, to your satisfaction, that your employees will respond by becoming far more conscientious.

Welch has tapped into something formidable here—the wish of every employee to feel that he or she is important to the company.

You too can exploit this. It will take some sacrifice on your part.

Managing less isn't always easy.

But, as we have seen in the case of Jack Welch, it has its advantages.

27

CREATE AN ATMOSPHERE WHERE EMPLOYEES FEEL FREE TO SPEAK OUT

FROM THE FILES OF

Jack Welch

"We have got to capture what happens here at Crotonville and push it across the whole company. We have to create an atmosphere where people can speak up to somebody who can do something about their problems."

One day in September 1988, Jack Welch was making a routine visit to Crotonville, GE's Management Development Institute.

There he was, standing in the Pit. In the audience were upper and lower levels of GE management.

The questions came fast and furious, different questions from the past.

Not about where he was taking the company. Not about how GE would fare in the near future. This time the questions were hard-hitting, specific ones about the businesses.

The speakers said they believed in General Electric's shared values. The trouble was their bosses did not.

One complainant griped the objective of downsizing and delayering might be correct. But the execution was lacking.

The goal may be to get rid of the less significant work. But that was not occurring.

The employees faced more demands from bosses and had less time than ever.

Another complainant asked: "If this is the best business in the world, then why do I go home feeling so miserable?"

Someone in the audience summed up the frustration that others felt:

> *When I'm here at Crotonville, I understand what you're saying. I have a chance to talk about it. I get it. But back home it's not like that. It's not happening that way. We don't have this kind of dialogue with our managers.*

The GE revolution had spawned an improved productivity rate—it was now at 4 to 5 percent, twice the earlier level.

The portfolios had been rearranged.

The brunt of the layoffs had occurred.

Yet the bosses remained, seemingly uncaring about their employees, expecting them to work harder than before, giving out tasks that seemed meaningless.

As always, Jack Welch was candid.

If he knew the answer, he gave it.

If he did not, he said simply, "I don't know. I hope you'll have the courage to ask that tough question of somebody who can do something about it when you go home."

Later Welch thought about that comment and the questions. He was annoyed at having heard the same questions asked over and over again in the Pit, questions that he felt should have been addressed back home in the businesses.

In the Pit, he had seemed repeatedly to be responding to the audience "I don't know," or "That's not my job; that's your job" or "I'm sorry, I don't know why you do that stupid thing, and why you don't fix this."

Why was there no dialogue within those businesses?

Welch thought for a moment.

Then he knew.

The answer was that General Electric remained hierarchic.

- Senior management talked only to junior management.

- Junior management talked only to subjunior management.

- And only subjunior management talked to the workers.

Workers were not expected to engage in dialogue with their superiors. They were simply expected to work.

Was it not time to end this chain-of-command rigidity?

Was it not time to harness the obvious energy and talent that existed among the employees who had asked those tough questions in the Pit that day?

The bosses who knew the answers to the questions raised in the Pit had to be forced to face their people and talk to them directly.

The effect would be to get the lower-level managers on board the GE revolution. The top managers were fine. But down below, despite delayering, there was still much hierarchy, too many unnecessary reports being filled out, too many managers still resistant to change.

Welch spoke to Jim Baughman, the Crotonville chief, about what he had in mind:

> **We have got to capture what happens here at Crotonville and push it across the whole company. We have to create an atmosphere where people can speak up to somebody who can do something about their problems.** *The reason these people say these unpleasant, difficult things to me is that they don't have an address. The trouble is, I can't impact on their lives. I hear what they say all right. But I go home. I get on the helicopter. I don't do something to fix their problems.*

Welch then thought of the solution.

If he had dealt with hardware in the first phase of his revolution, now it was time to deal with the software, the people.

Welch sensed that the hundreds of thousands of GE employees who were both frustrated and willing to share their ideas presented an opportunity.

Why not exploit that?

The question was how.

Crotonville's seminars were not enough. That much was clear. Nor were the videotapes that business leaders sent to employees. Nor were the once-a-year speeches the business leaders gave.

The time had come for managers and workers to talk with one another. The time had come for managers and workers to explore ways of improving the day-to-day workings of the business.

Just as Jack Welch had left his desk to stand in the Pit, he wanted GE's business leaders to go eyeball to eyeball with employees.

Sure there were definite risks for senior management.

General Electric had prided itself on knowing how the company should be run. It had written the book on management strategies for years.

Was it truly prepared to turn over the "managing" of the company from the qualified managers to the unqualified "soldiers"?

What were managers for if not to manage?

Jack Welch was ready to take the risk.

He did not believe managers had a monopoly on ideas.

He did not believe GE managers necessarily had a monopoly on solutions for day-to-day problems.

Indeed, he sensed that most of the creativity and innovation, which drove productivity, lay in the men and women closest to the actual work.

It was that creativity and innovation, that knowledge of what problems existed and how best to fix them, that encouraged Jack Welch to come up with a plan to liberate the worker.

It made good business sense, and it fit neatly into the scheme of what America was all about.

America, Welch liked to say, had the most free enterprise in the world. Only Britain came close.

> *What the US system has is freedom. It allows people like me to become chairman of GE in one generation. It allows the talented young engineers in our company to move up fast. If we put bureaucracy and rigidity into our system, we play into our competitors' hands in global markets. Because we don't get the benefits of the protected markets, the government support, the presidential relationships. But if we let our people flourish and grow, if we use the best ideas they come up with, then we have the chance to win.*
>
> *Our urge to liberate and empower the GE workforce is not enlightenment—it's a competitive necessity. When you look at the global arena, that's what our competitive advantage is. We have got to unleash it.*

Work-Out is Jack Welch's ambitious 10-year program that pushes cultural change throughout GE.

It began in 1989. It is an attempt to expand the notion of debate throughout the entire company.

Other companies have experimented with a number of the ideas that go into Work-Out. GE, however, was the first company to use them on such a large scale.

By early 1994 virtually all GE's employees had taken part in Work-Out.

Work-Out does many things. One of them is to redefine the notion of management. It is now part of a manager's task to listen to the views of his employees.

Work-Out aims in large measure to help Welch create what he calls the boundaryless company.

Work-Out, in Welch's words, was meant to help people stop

wrestling with the boundaries, the absurdities that grow in large organizations. We're all familiar with those absurdities: too many approvals, duplication, pomposity, waste.

28

LISTEN TO THE PEOPLE WHO ACTUALLY DO THE WORK!

29

ELIMINATE UNNECESSARY WORK!

FROM THE FILES OF

Jack Welch

*"O*ur desire to tap into this creativity . . . to listen more clearly to these ideas . . . and draw more of them out all over the company . . . led us to a process we call Work-Out."

Jack Welch was ready to liberate the workforce.

Welch had four important goals in mind in developing Work-Out:

1. DEVELOPING TRUST

- An employee would have to feel comfortable speaking out to a boss.

- He or she would have to be able to speak frankly without worrying about being dismissed.

- That candor would permit the company to benefit from the knowledge and ideas contained inside the heads of these employees.

2. EMPOWERING EMPLOYEES

- Those closest to the work are more knowledgeable about it than their bosses.

- The single best way of having these workers pass on that knowledge to their superiors was to give them more power.

- In exchange for that power, an employee would be expected to assume more responsibility in his or her job.

3. ELIMINATING UNNECESSARY WORK

- Higher productivity is a crucial goal.

- So too, however, is jettisoning tasks that no one can justify.

- Getting rid of those tasks would provide employees with some fast, understandable dividends from the Work-Out program.

4. SPREADING THE GE CULTURE

- Work-Out would, once it is adopted throughout the company, help in defining and fostering the new business culture that Jack Welch wants to create, one that is boundaryless, and has its workers seeking speed, simplicity, and self-confidence.

Welch began thinking of the details.

Employees had to be able to make suggestions to their bosses face to face. That was crucial.

And they had to be able to get a response—on the spot, if possible.

THE WALL OF HOSTILITY HAD TO COME DOWN.

The New England town meeting, which provided local citizens with a forum for dialogue with city fathers, seemed like an applicable model.

GENERAL ELECTRIC WAS GOING TO HOLD TOWN MEETINGS!

They would occur in all its businesses. The meetings would last three days.

Attending would be a cross section of GE's personnel—senior and junior managers, salaried and hourly workers—50 people or so at a time.

To break the ice, to get the ball rolling, to "facilitate" the dialogue, outside consultants and academics with expertise in business organization would be present.

Their task would be to:

ENCOURAGE THE AUDIENCE TO SPEAK OUT FRANKLY.

The business leader speaks first. He describes the particular business, its strengths, its weaknesses. He explains how it fits into the overall General Electric strategy.

Over the next two days, members of the audience are asked to evaluate four aspects of their business:

Reports.

Meetings.

Measurements.

Approvals.

WHICH OF THESE MADE SENSE?

WHICH DID NOT?

What could be eliminated so the business shot itself in the foot a little less? The idea was:

GET PEOPLE TALKING.

Get them talking about the easy issues, "the low-hanging fruit" in Jim Baughman's neat phrase.

Get them voicing their views on the issues that could be picked off without too much effort.

These were the nonsense habits that, with no one questioning their worth, had accumulated over the years and slowed productive work.

As employees grew comfortable in confronting the boss, the level of candor was supposed to increase.

That would allow tougher issues to be kicked around.

The object of the whole exercise:

GET MORE SPEED, SIMPLICITY, AND SELF-CONFIDENCE
INTO THE GE OPERATION.

Speed.

Simplicity.

Self-Confidence.

Those three ideas became the main goals of
JACK WELCH'S WORKERS REVOLUTION.

All of this needed a name.

Jack Welch sought to convey the idea of getting the nonsense "worked out" of General Electric.

He wanted to convey the "workout" that people engage in to make themselves lean and agile.

He wanted to convey the idea of dealing with problems that had to be "worked out."

AND SO HE CALLED THE PROGRAM WORK-OUT.

Some mistakenly thought the name was meant to justify further downsizing. Was Work-Out just another fancy name for "taking out" people?

No, insisted Welch.

In time, both the plan to create internal dialogue at forums within the company and the effort to import ideas from the outside came to be known as Work-Out.

Here is what Work-Out has done, in Jack Welch's words:

> *As we took down much of the clutter and scaffolding of layers and organizational structure . . . and got rid of the useless noise bureaucracy always generates . . . we started to see deeper into the organization . . . and hear the voices of those who actually did the work . . . ran the processes . . . and dealt with the customers. They had some striking ideas on how things could be done better.*

Our desire to tap into this creativity ... to listen more clearly to these ideas ... and draw more of them out all over the company ... led us to a process we call Work-Out.

Work-Out is many things ... meetings ... teams ... training ... but its central objective is growing a culture where everyone's ideas have value ... everyone plays a part ... where leaders lead rather than control ... coach rather than kibitz. Work-Out is the process of mining the creativity and productivity that we know resides in the American work force ... the most creative ... but irreverent ... the most energetic, but independent ... workforce in the world.

LEADERSHIP SECRET

30

GO BEFORE YOUR WORKERS
AND ANSWER ALL THEIR QUESTIONS!

FROM THE FILES OF
Jack Welch

*"**P**eople who had never been asked for any-thing other than their time and their hands now saw their minds, their views sought after. And in listening to their ideas, it became even more clear to everyone that the people who are closest to the work really do know it better."*

By early 1994 almost all GE's employees had participated in Work-Out.

Some 20,000 were taking part in the program on any given day at the company.

The "town meetings" started in March 1989. Those attending included hourly and salaried employees.

Employees and managers alike were asked to dress casually—chinos, T-shirts. The idea was to blur distinctions between managers and workers.

Three days were devoted to the session, usually held at an off-site conference center.

At the outset, the session was off limits to the boss.

Not only did the boss have to stay away, but he or she was also told that interfering with the session could jeopardize the boss's career.

On the third day, the boss was invited into the session to confront employees.

Work-Out rules required that the manager give answers to questions on the spot. As a result, 80 percent of the questions were given immediate answers. If a question needed study, the manager had to come up with an answer within a month.

At first the invisible walls between the two groups still loomed large, inhibiting the desired free-flowing conversation.

Then, in one session after another, it happened.

Someone would screw up his or her courage—and talk.

A question would be asked. A problem would be raised. It was as easy—and as hard—as that.

To the crowd's surprise, the manager listened.

Quietly. Patiently.

The manager seemed genuinely sympathetic, not at all bothered that one of the privates was challenging a major.

Once the ice had broken, someone else in the audience caught on. His or her hand went up.

Again the manager listened—and responded. Right then and there. On the spot.

Soon hands were raised all around the room.

Not every experience went smoothly. Union members shared a natural suspicion when company executives came forward with a proposal—any proposal—and wanted to sit down and talk about it.

Work-Out, of course, was no ordinary proposal. This was a proposal to turn over decision-making power to the workers. To union members, there seemed every good reason to be a little suspicious.

The union people listened, however.

Sometimes senior managers appeared to have trouble explaining themselves. That led to even more suspicion.

The Work-Out program began at GE's Schenectady operation in the fall of 1990. Hourly workers were pulled out of shops. The first sessions did not go well.

To the union members who attended, Work-Out appeared little more than a glorified opportunity for workers to squeal on one another. Someone had tattled on a person who read the newspaper when he should have been working. Someone else had accused an associate of "hiding behind his machine" all day.

Was it possible to prevent the town meetings from degenerating into nothing more than a "rat session"?

Was it possible to keep the meetings from turning into nothing more productive than pointing out who was lazy or who was calling the boss an idiot?

That became a major test of the program.

In time, at Schenectady and elsewhere, GE's union members began to sense that management's purpose was to get out of bad work habits, not simply to uncover laggards.

At early Work-Out sessions in GE Supply, the participants broke work issues into two categories. They called them **"rattlers" and "pythons."**

Someone noted that **rattlers** made a good deal of noise and were immediately recognizable. It was therefore easy to find and shoot them.

Pythons, however, made no noise and lay entwined in trees. Thus it was far more difficult to eradicate them.

These two categories appeared to represent GE neatly.

Like pythons entwined in trees, the company was often tied up in knots by its bureaucracy. The idea was to untie the knots by attacking a variety of problems—easy and hard.

The easy problems that could be solved at once were called the **rattlers. Pythons** were the hard problems that need more time and effort.

Here's an example of a rattler.

It occurred at a factory where a young woman who put out a popular and well-received plant newspaper had encountered a key frustration that she had kept to herself.

She waited for a Work-Out session to fire away at her boss.

> *"Look," she said after raising her hand at a town meeting of her business, "it takes me seven signatures every month to get my plant newspaper released. You all like the plant newspaper. It's never been criticized. It's won awards. Why does it take seven signatures?"*

Her boss looked at her in amazement. "This is crazy. I didn't know that was the case."

"Well, that's the way it is," she replied.

"OK," the general manager said, "from now on, no more signatures."

The newspaper editor smiled.

A rattler. A relatively easy one. A problem that was easily recognizable. And therefore, it could be fixed on the spot.

And it was.

Here's an example of **another rattler**. It comes from a factory worker speaking at a town meeting.

> *I've worked for GE for over 20 years. I have a perfect attendance record. I've won management awards. I love this company. It's put my kids through college. It's given me a good standard of living. But there's something stupid that I'd like to bring up.*

His work, operating a valuable piece of equipment, required him to wear gloves. The gloves wore out several times a month.

To acquire another pair he had to call in a relief operator or, if none was available, shut his machine down. He then had to walk to another building, go to the supply room, and fill out a form. Then he had to track down a supervisor of sufficient authority to countersign his request.

Only after he returned the countersigned form to the supply room was he given a new pair of gloves. Frequently he lost as much as an hour of work.

"I think it's stupid."

"I think it's stupid too," said his general manager, who was standing in front of the room. "Why do we do that?"

From the rear came the answer: "In 1979 we lost a box of gloves."

"Put the box of gloves on the floor, close to the people," the manager ordered.

Another rattler shot.

At the Research and Development Center in Schenectady, an employee attending a Work-Out session asked why managers were given special parking places.

No one could think of a good reason. The managerial privilege was rescinded.

At a Work-Out session for the company's communications personnel, a secretary asked why she had to interrupt her own work to empty the out tray on her boss's desk. Why, on his trips outside his office, could he not drop the material on her desk?

No one had a good answer. So a few steps of unproductive effort were scratched from the secretary's routine.

At a Work-Out session involving GE's power generation personnel, someone noted the purchasing department chose welding equipment without consulting the welders who used it. Accordingly, equipment inappropriate for certain tasks had sometimes been selected.

Why not have welders join the purchasing team when it visited vendors to order equipment?

The manager did not hesitate. "Fine," he said.

Changing such procedures—eliminating the seven signatures needed for the newspaper, removing parking privileges for managers, or even asking bosses to empty their own out trays—required little time or study to implement.

These were all examples of the low-hanging fruit that was easy to pick.

As employees dealt with even the trivial, easy issues, Work-Out was giving them an increased sense of participation in their jobs and a good feeling about themselves.

LEADERSHIP SECRET

31

AIM FOR SPEED, SIMPLICITY, AND SELF-CONFIDENCE!

FROM THE FILES OF Jack Welch

"The biggest mistake we could make right now is to think that simply doing more of what worked in the 80s will be enough to win the 90s. It won't."

"The way to get faster, more productive, and more competitive is to unleash the energy and intelligence and raw, ornery self-confidence of the American worker, who is still by far the most productive and innovative in the world."

In the late 1980s and early 90s, Jack Welch began to think about the kind of company General Electric should become in the future.

Articulating that dream, he was in effect offering a prescription for the way all large American corporations ought to behave.

In September 1989 he noted:

The 80s have forced business to change. The complacent and timid had a date with hostile takeover people. Ten million manufacturing jobs were eliminated and shifted to the service sector. Seventeen million new jobs were created, and unemployment dropped to its lowest point in 15 years. American firms began to globalize. The results of the 80s show that things worked.

The biggest mistake we could make right now is to think that simply doing more of what worked in the 80s will be enough to win the 90s. It won't. Productivity still lags behind Japan despite major gains in the 80s. And the competitive arena is much tougher and complex. Whereas at the start of the 80s, Japan was the one powerful competitor, today it is Europe and Korea and Taiwan. Korea and Taiwan, once sourcing areas for labor-intensive electronic products, are now major manufacturing powerhouses in electronics, autos, steel, and many other industries. Others in the Far East are following in their paths.

Simply going after more of the hardware solutions that worked in the 80s will just not be enough to win in the 90s.

The point is—the competitive world of the 90s will make the 80s look like a walk in the park.

How does America win the 90s?

To win we have to find the key to dramatic, sustained productivity growth . . .

We have to turn in the 90s—to the software of our companies—to the culture that drives them.

To change the culture in a fundamental way meant, according to Jack Welch:

- Looking beyond incentive plans.

- Looking beyond a hundred other suggestions from the how-to books.

- Looking beyond the hero of the week who single-handedly saves or transforms a company.

We have to move from the incremental to the radical, toward a fundamental revolution in our approach to productivity and to work itself—a revolution that must touch every single person in the organization every business day.

Jack Welch summed up his prescription in three words:

SPEED

SIMPLICITY

SELF-CONFIDENCE

Speed occurred when people made decisions in minutes, face to face, and avoided producing months of staff work or forests of paper.

> *We found in the 80s that speed increases in an organization as control decreases. We had constructed over the years a management apparatus that was right for its times, the toast of the business schools. Divisions, strategic business units, groups, sectors, all were designed to make meticulous, calculated decisions and move them smoothly forward and upward. This system produced highly polished work. It was right for the 70s . . . a growing handicap in the early 80s . . . and it would have been a ticket to the boneyard in the 90s.*
>
> *So we got rid of it . . . When we did this we began to see people . . . who for years had spent half their time serving the system and the other half fighting it . . . suddenly come to life, making decisions in minutes, but this transformation, this rebirth, was largely confined to upper management. In the 90s we want to see it engulf and galvanize the entire company.*

Simplicity had numerous definitions:

> *To an engineer it's clean, functional designs with fewer parts. For manufacturing it means judging a process not by how sophisticated it is, but how understandable it is to those who must make it work. In marketing it means clear messages and clean proposals to consumers and industrial customers. And, most importantly, on an individual, interpersonal level it takes the form of plain-speaking, directness—honesty.*

Simplicity was also essential for a leader's most important function—

PROJECTING A VISION.

The leader's unending responsibility must be to remove every detour, every barrier to ensure that vision is first clear and then real. The leader must create an atmosphere in the organization where people feel not only free to, but obliged to, demand clarity and purpose from their leaders.

Simplicity is an indispensable element of a leader's most important functions: projecting a vision and demanding and rewarding boldness . . . speed . . . and passion . . . as his or her people move closer to it.

SELF-CONFIDENCE

It takes enormous self-confidence to be simple—particularly in large organizations. Self-confidence does not grow in someone who is just another appendage on the bureaucracy, whose authority rests on little more than a title. Bureaucracy is terrified by speed and hates simplicity. It fosters defensiveness, intrigue, sometimes meanness. Those who are trapped in it are afraid to share, can't be passionate, and—in the 90s—won't win.

A company cannot distribute **self-confidence**. But it can provide opportunities to dream, risk, and win and hence to earn **self-confidence**.

Speed. Simplicity. Self-confidence. *We can grow a work ethic that plays to our strengths, one that unleashes and liberates the awesome productive energy* *that we know resides in our workforce. If we can let people see that what they do counts, means something; if you and I and the business leadership of the country can have the self-confidence to let people go—to create an environment where each man and woman who works in our companies can see a clear connection between what he or she does every day, all day, and winning and losing in the real world—we can become productive beyond our wildest dreams—certainly beyond the abilities of our international competitors, most of whom are hobbled by cultures that make it virtually impossible for them to liberate and empower their people.*

Our natural strong suit is the energy and creativity of an irreverent, aggressive, impatient, and curious people. It is ours to win with—if we can shift gears from decades of controlling things to a decade of liberating— turning people loose to dream, dare, and win.

Believing that the defense industries of the 90s would experience problems similar to those that the rust belt business suffered in the 80s, Welch said:

Accepting this reality was the first step in dealing with it—and rightsizing is the second. Only those who move quickly to resize themselves will survive and prosper in the 90s.

Education, Welch asserted, was a great challenge for the 90s.

If we ask our employees at every level of the workforce to win in a world seething with change, we must provide them with the tools to do so.

In December 1991 Welch answered the question "What I Want US Business to Do in '92?" He was writing, along with other leaders in commerce, politics, religion, and academic life, in *Fortune* magazine.

> *The job all of us have in business is to flatten the building and break down the walls. If we do that, we will be getting more people coming up with more ideas for the action items that a business needs to work with.*
>
> *Not every idea is a capital "I" idea. A breakthrough in biotech—that's the wrong view of an idea. An idea is an error-free billing system. An idea is taking a process that requires six days and getting it done in one. Everyone can contribute—every single person. The people who process the work in general have better ideas than those in the office, far better ideas. The key is to give them respect, dignity. When you spend three days in a room with people mapping a process, the ideas just about bubble up inside. Just give them respect—everybody in the organization—and the improvement is enormous.*

Increasing **productivity** remained Welch's chief concern in the early 1990s. He sensed that despite his late 80s efforts to remove management layers and other features of bureaucracy, much more work of this kind needed to be done. As he wrote in the 1991 annual report:

> *Unfortunately, it is still possible to find documents around GE businesses that look like something out of the National Archives, with 5, 10, or even more signatures necessary before action can be taken. In some businesses you might still encounter many layers of management in a small area—boiler operators reporting to*

the supervisor of boilers, who reports to the utility manager, who reports to the manager of plant services, who reports to the plant manager, and so on.

Welch wanted more **delayering**.

He spelled out in the summer of 1992 what he hoped would be his legacy for GE:

> *I would like to think that we created a world-class company where our reputation for excellence is everything. That what we do is well accepted on every continent. That we (have on the GE team) an excited, involved group of people who take part in a meritocracy, who have enriched their lives and their family's lives, who won big by participating in this modern corporation where everyone has a stake, everyone is a participant, that by involving everyone in the process to create this well-respected, leadership, global company (we have won).*

In a speech he gave to the General Electric Annual Meeting of Share Owners in Fort Wayne, Indiana, on April 28, 1993, Welch explained that, while **boundarylessness** makes strong global businesses even stronger and puts them even further ahead of their competition, one other form of business behavior is even more critical. And that is

INVOLVING EVERYBODY.

While General Electric's appliance business has been profitable, its headquarters location at Louisville has had a significant cost disadvantage in relation to its competitors. The plant is losing money and Welch acknowledges, "We can't stay there" unless total costs are brought down.

This is where **involving everybody** comes in.

The only solution is to draw more ideas, better ideas, not just from a few, but from every single individual in that plant. And we've begun to do just that with all the numbers on the table—all the books open—all options discussed—and every person in the place contributing his or her ideas and energy toward a win for us all.

Whether we win or lose in Louisville remains to be seen, but what is certain is that there will not be a man or woman in our Louisville operations who will not have access to all the facts—or will not have a chance to contribute to winning.

To Welch, the critical component of a business is **people**.

We are determined to build a culture in General Electric where 200,000-plus people will come to work in search of a better way—every day. Because while strategy and technology and market development and acquisitions and dispositions and the rest of the business "stuff" are important, putting them all together comes back to people. GE wins or loses with people.

The companies that find a way to engage every mind—harness every volt of passionate energy, bring excitement to the lives of the people, and break every artificial barrier between people—will be the companies that win in the '90s and beyond.

In June 1993 Welch had this to say about the 1990s:

I said the 90s would make the 80s a walk in the park. I underestimated that by a factor of 10 . . . Because we had global growth in the late 80s everywhere we built large capacity, then we globalized, and we made the world accessible to one another. Then the world stopped growing, so demand is way out of whack on a global scale. So you're going to have pressures in the 90s on margins and costs that are going to make three years ago look like a joke. The pressure on competitiveness is going to be escalated about two more notches . . . So if companies can't get productivity, it's going to be incredible. They're going to wither again.

In short, Jack Welch believes that the key to competitive advantage in the 1990s will be:

THE CAPACITY OF LEADERSHIP TO CREATE A LEARNING ENVIRONMENT THAT IS CAPABLE OF CREATING INTELLECTUAL CAPITAL COMPRISING IDEAS AND INNOVATION.

TABLE A

The following "GE Values" have become General Electric's credo for the 1990s. These values develop out of Jack Welch's 31 leadership secrets.

- Create a clear, simple, reality-based, customer-focused vision and be able to communicate it straightforwardly to all constituencies.

- Understand accountability and commitment and be decisive . . . set and meet aggressive targets . . . always with unyielding integrity.

- Have a passion for excellence . . . hate bureaucracy and all the nonsense that comes with it.

- Have the self-confidence to empower others and behave in a boundaryless fashion . . . believe in and be committed to Work-Out as a means of empowerment . . . be open to ideas from anywhere.

- Have, or have the capacity to develop, global brains and global sensitivity and be comfortable building diverse global teams.

- Stimulate and relish change . . . do not be frightened or paralyzed by it. See change as opportunity, not just a threat.

- Have enormous energy and the ability to energize and invigorate others. Understand speed as a competitive advantage and see the total organizational benefits that can be derived from a focus on speed.

The 360° leadership assessment chart used by GE provides a basis to grade employees from all directions (e.g., manager, peers, direct reports, and customers). The chart reflects GE's values.

Documents to Live By: GEIPS 360° Leadership Assessment

Characteristic	Performance Criteria	Mgr.	Peers	Subor-dinates	Other
Vision	• Has developed and communicated a clear, simple, customer-focused vision/direction for the organization.				
	• Forward-thinking, stretches horizons, challenges imaginations.				
	• Inspires and energizes others to commit to Vision. Captures minds. Leads by example.				
	• As appropriate, updates Vision to reflect constant and accelerating change impacting the business.				

Customer/ Quality Focus	● Listens to customer and assigns the highest priority to customer satisfaction, including internal customers. ● Inspires and demonstrates a passion for excellence in every aspect of work. ● Strives to fulfill commitment to Quality in total product/ service offering. ● Lives Customer Service and creates service mind-set throughout organization.
Integrity	● Maintains unequivocal commitment to honesty/truth in every facet of behavior. ● Follows through on commitments; assumes responsibility for own mistakes. ● Practices absolute conformance with company policies embodying GEI&PS commitment to ethical conduct. ● Actions and behaviors are consistent with words. Absolutely trusted by others.
Accountability/ Commitment	● Sets and meets aggressive commitments to achieve business objectives. ● Demonstrates courage/self-confidence to stand up for beliefs, ideas, co-workers. ● Fair and compassionate yet willing to make difficult decisions. ● Demonstrates uncompromising responsibility for preventing harm to the environment.

(continued)

Characteristic	Performance Criteria	Mgr.	Peers	Subordinates	Other
Communication/Influence	● Communicates in open, candid, clear, complete, and consistent manner—invites response/dissent. ● Listens effectively and probes for new ideas. ● Uses facts and rational arguments to influence and persuade. ● Breaks down barriers and develops influential relationships across teams, functions, and layers.				
Shared Ownership/ Boundaryless	● Self-confidence to share information across traditional boundaries and be open to new ideas. ● Encourages/promotes shared ownership for Team Vision and goals. ● Trusts others; encourages risk taking and boundaryless behavior. ● Champions Work-Out as a vehicle for everyone to be heard. Open to ideas from anywhere.				
Team Builder/ Empowerment	● Selects talented people; provides coaching and feedback to develop team members to fullest potential. ● Delegates whole tasks; empowers team to maximize effectiveness. Is personally a Team Player. ● Recognizes and rewards achievement. Creates positive/ enjoyable work environment. ● Fully utilizes diversity of team members (cultural, race, gender) to achieve business success.				

_____

_____

_____

**Knowledge/
Expertise/
Intellect**

- Possesses and readily shares functional/technical knowledge and expertise. Constant interest in learning.
- Demonstrates broad business knowledge/perspective with cross-functional/multicultural awareness.
- Makes good decisions with limited data. Applies intellect to the fullest.
- Quickly sorts relevant from irrelevant information, grasps essentials of complex issues and initiates action.

**Initiative/
Speed**

- Creates real and positive change. Sees change as an Opportunity.
- Anticipates problems and initiates new and better ways of doing things.
- Hates/avoids/eliminates "bureaucracy" and strives for brevity, simplicity, clarity.
- Understands and uses speed as a competitive advantage.

**Global
Mind-Set**

- Demonstrates global awareness/sensitivity and is comfortable building diverse/global teams.
- Values and promotes full utilization of global and work force diversity.
- Considers the global consequences of every decision. Proactively seeks global knowledge.
- Treats everyone with dignity, trust, and respect.

RATING SCALE: Significant Development Need 1 2 3 4 5 Outstanding Strength

Other books of interest to you from Irwin Professional Publishing . . .

BOGLE ON MUTUAL FUNDS

New Perspectives for the Intelligent Investor

John C. Bogle

A Fortune Book® Club Main Selection!
The "father of the index fund" and a "crusader" of the industry shares his wealth of wisdom and expertise, explaining not only the basic principles of mutual fund investing, but also the unique nuances and subtleties of this alluring field. (300 pages)
ISBN: 1-55623-860-6

THE NEW GE

How Jack Welch Revived an American Institution

Robert Slater

Through rare and exclusive interviews with Jack Welch and dozens of GE insiders, internationally renowned *Time* magazine reporter Robert Slater gives an inside look at General Electric and the bold leader responsible for GE's magic. (295 pages)
ISBN: 1-55623-670-0

THE DISNEY TOUCH

How a Daring Management Team Revived an Entertainment Empire

Ron Grover

Grover, one of Hollywood's best business reporters, reveals how Michael Eisner, Frank Wells, and the members of Team Disney engineered the turnaround that continues to amaze businesspeople everywhere. (250 pages)
ISBN: 1-55623-385-X

THE SECRET EMPIRE
How 25 Multinationals Rule the World
Janet Lowe

Reveals the global giants who are often more influential than the countries in which they operate! Lowe identifies the leading multinationals, describing what they do, their corporate personalities, and who runs them. (335 pages)
ISBN: 1-55623-513-5

SECOND TO NONE
How Our Smartest Companies Put People First
Charles Garfield

This best-selling author offers an inside look at today's leading businesses and how they became masters at expanding the teamwork and creativity of their employees. (452 pages)
ISBN: 1-55623-360-4

Available at fine bookstores and libraries everywhere.